Ashley,

I hope these poems witness to the courage, resilience, and decency of the Iraqi and

With Children Like Your Own

Afghan people I've met.

Wishing you well with your art and your studies —

David

September, 2011

WITH CHILDREN
LIKE YOUR OWN

Iraq and Afghanistan Poems, 2008–2011

David Smith-Ferri

Foreword by Kathy Kelly

Haley's
Athol, Massachusetts

Haley's
488 South Main Street
Athol, MA 01331
haley.antique@verizon.net
800.215.8805

Special thanks to Mary-Ann DeVita Palmieri, copy editor, and to Jane Cadarette.

International Standard Book Number: 978-1-884540-28-8

Library of Congress Catalogue Number: 2011928758

For the Afghan Youth Peace Volunteers
and for my friends at Direct Aid Iraq

Contents

A Promise that the Darkness Will Lift

a foreword by Kathy Kelly

During an October, 2010 visit to Afghanistan, David Smith-Ferri, Jerica Arents, and I spent a week with Afghan Youth Peace Volunteers, an organization of brave youngsters between eleven and twenty-one who welcomed us into their mountain village homes in Afghanistan's Bamiyan province. Bamiyan, once site of famous colossal Buddhas that fell casualty to recent Afghan discord, is now one of few places in Afghanistan where there is relative calm. The peace volunteers arranged for us to stay in a guest house on the main street while they occupied a small tent on the outskirts of the tiny town. On our final night, they served us dinner outside the tent and then invited us inside for a farewell gathering. There David read, by flashlight, from Battlefield without Borders, his first book—the predecessor to the volume you now hold—poems about embattled Iraqis and how they have borne (or failed to bear) the terrible brunt of siege, warfare, and displacement.

An expectant hush pervaded the tent. David started by reading to us of Mustafa, whose body was broken beyond repair when a bomb blast threw him off the roof of his Baghdad home. Mustafa had waited out the 2003 invasion and then eagerly carried a satellite dish to his rooftop, hoping at last to break out of years of enforced isolation ordained by United Nations sanctions instigated by the United States. What he broke instead—what US ordnance broke—was his spine. Years later, David met Mustafa in Jordan and learned of his terrible isolation, his cruelly difficult struggle as a wheelchair-bound man seeking health care and resettlement in the middle of a war. And so through David's verses, we in the tent also came to know Mustafa.

I watched the rapt young Afghans nodding their heads, drawn into Mustafa's tale of pain and struggle. Their own memories and experiences shared by their loved ones made such a story, sadly, commonplace for them. For them, even unusual heroism like Mustafa's is familiar, not so unusual. I knew that the boys themselves, so tremendously brave, would soon figure as subjects in David's poems. The flashlights illuminating their faces there in the dark tent would be augmented for Western readers back home who would peer through the dark of these times aided by the light of my friend David's gifts for exquisite language, image, and metaphor. And so, we might share in their courage.

When the stories David heard were harsh and terrifying, as from Afghan refugees we would later meet, I thought of how he would illuminate them. Squatting before mud-and-tarpaulin huts in a Kabul refugee camp, David does not avert his eyes from the people before him. He sees, and so we see, the people and their children, mired against their will in dirt. He listens and brings to his mind's eye children who aren't there, the ones who have been killed, who are covered in soil. And so, we see those children, too, their parents' tightly-held, half-crumpled photos attesting to the cost of nine years of unseeing, of our national refusal to listen, of US raids and drone strikes.

There is so much dark. It is not possible to read these poems and remain unmoved. They link us with our brothers and sisters who have suffered and still suffer. And listening is not enough. But it is the beginning and the early tremor of seismic energy unleashed when those who yearn for peace and freedom join together.

In the aftermath of the killing of Osama bin Laden, my thoughts turn to what had been suggested as alternatives to invading Afghanistan. One response was that the US and other countries could enact a criminal investigation and rely on police work and intelligence to apprehend the perpetrators of the attack. As it turns out, the US discovered where Osama bin Laden was through those means and not through warfare. How have the past ten years of aerial bombardments, night raids, death squads, assassinations, and drone attacks in Afghanistan benefited the US people? Did the carnage and bloodshed bring the US closer to discovering the whereabouts of Osama bin Laden? Have we defeated terrorism or created greater, deeper hatred toward the US?

Dr. Martin Luther King, Jr. once called for a neighborliness that goes beyond one's tribe, race, class, and nation. We think of that call when we remember what happened when David, others, and I visited another rural village in the central highlands of Afghanistan in 2010. We sat with women who were close in age to the young people who were celebrating outside of the White House after Osama bin Laden was killed. Asked if they had ever heard of a time when a large passenger plane had crashed into a tall building in the United States, the young Afghan women were puzzled. They had never heard of 9/11. And, again, David listened, and his poetry helps us to understand.

David's poems lack the cool and comforting detachment of military accounts that tidy lives into timelines and deaths into benchmarks that make it possible to listen without hearing as statistics impose a particular order designed to conceal the chaos, violence, and upheaval of war. David instead calls forth the clenched fear seizing war's ravaged victims. His words insist that we watch a beloved child slipping from his father's grasp as the bullet slips through them both. We can't escape the dread faced by the dying man. We must breathe the lethal metallic fumes of old bomb smoke and see the children in Iraqi and Afghan cancer wards. As it always should be, truth about warfare is told here through children; the cost, after all, is paid by them. Truth shows in the eyes of parents who can no longer feed and house their children, who know with a terrible understanding that they can no longer hope to keep their children safe. These are families torn apart by the all-too-real tearing of the bomb blast and by the grip of fears borne of war, threats, abandonment, mistrust.

And poverty. When David is in Amman, Jordan, with Noah Baker Merrill, a co-founder of Direct Aid Iraq, they are visiting families of hungry, sick Iraqi refugees unwanted in Jordan—or elsewhere, for that matter. Their lives left behind, they exist in squalor, in hovels. As David recounts the story, Noah, stricken by what he has seen, dissolves in tears. Haider, a refugee, grips Noah's arm and says, "We need you to be strong. And we need you to be smart and to stay with us, because soon the world is going to forget all about us." There is much in this book that brings me close to tears, but now David is grabbing my arm, and he will not let me blur truth with tears. David will not let me look away.

There is so much to look for and to connect. The brave young men in the tent in Afghanistan look toward Egypt with hope and longing. They have heard David's closing reflection about those who for decades have struggled to raise tents like the ones used in nonviolent protest by the courageous occupiers of Tahrir Square. He prefaces his poem "We are Here to Stay" with words from Hossam Moussa, 41, an accountant. Hossam told a Bloomberg News reporter, on February 9, 2011, that he came to Tahrir Square with his son after work every day. "I feel it's important," said Hossam, "for him to see for himself what it takes to build a better future."

With Children Like Your Own calls us to envision a world where people everywhere enter the metaphorical listening tent to answer invitations to talk and hear and, thus, to find their way out of a violent present into a peaceful future, through the darkness into the dawn.

And so David listens. He listens to stories that no one would want to hear, but he hears. David hears of horrible cruelty and the unfathomable ugliness of war, and yet his poems speak to us with incredible beauty. Surely, it is his skill. But it is also his perception of the beauty of parents' love, the beauty of brave young people in their Bamiyan tent, the beauty that shines in darkness and offers a promise that the darkness will lift.

These poems invite you to look and listen. These are "children like your own," and it's painful to watch such glowing hearts threatened by such dark. Please don't avert your eyes, please let these children teach you. Please let the artistry of David's language, and the simpler beauty of his poet's heart, carry you through the nightmares we have created in Iraq, in Afghanistan, and wherever we wage our wars.

Choreography

from Ukiah, California
May, 2011, after Osama bin Laden is killed

I
Though we know it is a play,
 the media role well-rehearsed—

though the news reporters are professional actors
performing under the glare of stage lights—

though the expert testimony is scripted,
the entire production directed, choreographed, and stage-managed,

we cannot turn off the radio or television,
we cannot leave the theater.

We cannot resist drinking the sweet, burgundy words
poured in crystal and placed in front of us.
We cannot take our lips from the glass.

II
In the same week that US-NATO missiles,
brilliantly directed,
kill Muammar Quaddafi's son and three grandchildren,
US Navy SEALs, playing their starring roles,
infiltrate a compound in Abottabad, Pakistan
and kill Osama bin Laden, his son, and two associates.

III
The cable networks bring out one cameo performer after another—
former intelligence officers,
military personnel,
elected officials—
and without exception
they greet the news with sun-ripened optimism,
laying flowers at the feet of US intelligence services,

US Special Operations,
the current and former White House administrations.

The whole operation, they tell us,
hung secretly on the vine, producing sugar.
The winemaker chose the exact moment to pick the fruit,
and the harvest is choice and sweet.

Over and over, they refer to the event as
the death of Osama bin Laden,
as though he had slipped on loose stone
while walking alone on a remote, steep, and tricky section of trail,
and though every effort was made to locate him,
the wound became infected,
and help arrived too late.

Not one of them says the word murder or assassination.
Few people notice when the scriptwriters and dramaturges
escort these words
out of the theater,
out of the city,
and take them, shackled and hooded,
to a secret detention center.

Apparently, in a country of three hundred million people,
there isn't a single member of the intelligentsia
who isn't convinced of the sugar level of this fruit,
how it ripened slowly, gathering flavor and distinction,
how it is sure to produce prize-winning wine.
One giddy NPR commentator,
crediting Barack Obama,
described it as
this wonderful American victory with Osama.

Taking their cue,
celebratory crowds coalesce in front of the White House

singing, cheering,
chanting USA, USA, USA
as though the national soccer team has just won the World Cup.
Not to be outdone, people swell Times Square.
Some even climb street lights and perch there spraying champagne.
All night, until the countervailing force
of a morning commute disperses them,
they hug and slap and kiss each other,
as though a war has ended
and the troops are coming home.
As though a promise, long withheld, has been kept,
and against all expectations a longed-for change has come.

IV
I walk into the hills behind my home.
Finches ride long-necked grasses,
eating their green seeds.
Deciduous oaks sprout hands and open them to sun and wind.
Carrying in its mind memories of the last ice age,
and in its body the strength of spring runoff,
Mill Creek thinks out loud.

All afternoon and into evening,
I listen to grasses,
trees,
water.

Nothing, they say, is *changed*.

Iraq

Direct Aid Iraq Team leader Najlaa Al-Nashi in Amman, Jordan
—photo by Tomiko Jones

This Is Not Old News

By mid-2007, when the "Iraqi Displacement Crisis" reached its peak, it was widely estimated that from four-and-a-half to five million Iraqis had fled their homes as a result of war and violence. About two-and-a-half million Iraqis had fled their country, the majority seeking refuge in neighboring Jordan and Syria. Another two million fled internally, to other parts of Iraq.

Iraqis living in Jordan and Syria had none of the legal protections that refugee status confers. They entered the country as visitors with short-term visas that soon expired. They were, literally, illegal. They had to fend for themselves. No refugee housing was established. They had no right to work. Those who did work risked imprisonment and deportation. Their children did not have the promise of free public schooling. Without the protections of citizenship or refugee status, their vulnerability was well known. They were subject to abuse by employers, landlords, police, and others.

In visits to Jordan in December, 2006 and in April, 2009, I met Iraqis who had been injured and had lost family members in U.S missile strikes, who had been imprisoned and tortured in US and Iraqi detention centers, who had fled death threats, who had been kidnapped, whose children had been kidnapped, whose businesses had been bombed or burned, whose homes had been seized. In short, I met people who had been living with war. Why are we so quick to accept our government's characterization of war as a means to peace and stability when there is so much evidence to the contrary, and the long-term effects of violence are so troubling and destabilizing?

The Iraqis I met in Jordan were not hapless victims but strong, resilient, courageous, and determined people. In exile Iraqis, often portrayed to the world as a hopelessly divided and brutal people, found and comforted each other. They organized themselves on behalf of the most vulnerable members of their communities, sharing scarce resources and advocating for services with the United Nations and international non-governmental organizations. This is one of the important underreported stories of our time. The supportive activity among Iraqis and underreporting continue today as does the suffering of displaced Iraqis.

Najlaa Al-Nashi, an Iraqi refugee living first in Syria and then Jordan, worked tirelessly to address immediate needs of Iraqis displaced by war. In January of 2007, when she met Americans Noah and Natalie Baker Merrill who were in Jordan reporting on the Iraqi Displacement Crisis, they discussed the possibility of Americans supporting Najlaa's work. What emerged over the next two-and-a-half years was an effort called Direct Aid Iraq (DAI), through which hundreds of Iraqis received direct medical aid, advocacy on a range of issues from resettlement to medical care, food, household furnishings, emotional support, and friendship.

This work was carried out under difficult and sometimes dangerous circumstances by a dedicated team of Iraqis. It was supported daily by a group of six Americans and by the generosity of peace groups and individuals across the US, especially Voices for Creative Nonviolence. Though it ended in late 2009 after Najlaa and other members of the Iraqi team resettled, DAI remains a model of providing effective humanitarian aid, one in which Americans play a supportive role by assisting indigenous leadership, talent, and networks.

The poems about Iraq in this book cover a range of issues and concerns and introduce people I met through Direct Aid Iraq, both Iraqi leaders of DAI who are my good friends and some of the Iraqi people who came to DAI for help.

Alive

Amman, Jordan
January, 2008

Mustafa Ahmed speaks

If you lie on the ground long enough
and very still,
the earth will swallow you.
Grass will grow on the spot.
A rock will replace you,
and mice will crouch in its shade.

This is what happened to my father and grandfather
outside our home in Baghdad when the SUV drove up,
the big car with its eyes closed.
How could they see us—
three branches of our family tree,
past, present, and future rooted in one place—
how could they see us through closed eyes?

The Sunni gunmen never stepped from their car,
never hailed us.
They had no legs or arms.
They are gunmen.
Their bodies, coiled on car seats,
darted like steel snakes through the windows,
sensing the air.
They could smell us.
Do Shia people have a different smell than Sunni people?

So many bullets.
But only one sound
like a mountain cracking,
a volcano of sound
and a thousand stone teeth biting us.
I did not have time to cover my face

or hide it in my father's shoulder,
only to fall from his arms to the ground.
It was the last time I touched him.

Before the bullets came, I was still part of his body.
When he wrapped me with his arms,
his body opened and took me in.
When he held me in one arm, at his waist,
my feet and legs grew, like a grafted branch, like a plant or tree in its
soil,
out of his hip.
But the bullets cut me off,
dug me out,
tore me from his side, snapping my roots.

The gunmen left me for dead,
left me like a stone,
part of my skull missing;
left me like a chipped or broken stone,
blue and red veins like minerals beneath its surface
exposed now and glistening in the sun.
The earth began to open around me,
to fold my two-year-old body into its mouth.
It did not happen all at once
but slowly,
my body sinking into soil, soon to become dirt.
Maybe I was dead already,
my bones softening, my back and shoulders already turning to soil.
Maybe I was already dead, when later,
in the dark, my aunt found me and folded me into her body.
Maybe she had to bring me back out of the earth,
out of the spirit world,
as my mother had when she gave birth to me.

And maybe I died again, last week,
in Jordan,

when my "Uncle Omar," my father's childhood friend,
an Iraqi medical doctor,
a Sunni,
brought me to a hospital in Amman.
Maybe I died when the Jordanian doctors put me under.
Maybe I was already turning into a white sheet and mattress
when they fitted a permanent plate in my skull
and Dr. Omar pronounced me alive
and gave me back to this world of arms and legs and voices.

Other Hands

Amman, Jordan
April, 2008

for the Direct Aid Iraq Team

Haifa'a speaks

Time to think.
Suddenly, in the midst of war,
time to remember,
to sift and re-sift,
to see clearly.

For fifty years, I lived by the sun's light,
drinking it through the mouth of my pupils.
Who could distinguish between that light and my eyes?
Didn't my eyes also glow,
weren't they themselves also stars?

For fifty years, my eyes and hands were lovers
lost in a loop,
one chasing the other.
Eyes leading,
hands following,
they mapped the world,
memorizing its shape, texture, mass, color,
knowing the actual thing— bread, water, soil, stone—
and loving its illuminated body.

But there is toxic light
that illuminates nothing.

All that intercourse ended
when incendiary bullets
like molten beetles

bored into my face.
They ate my right eye.
They ate the bone beneath it.
Banning sunlight,
breaking a fifty-year-old circuit of love,
they burned my other eye.

Who first imagined phosphorous weapons,
their molten hunger?
Who dreamed of one light eating another,
of light eclipsing the love of light?

When the phosphorous munitions struck my face,
when they began to melt my skin and bone and eyeball,
my hands could do nothing.
My hands could not shield, could not lead my eyes away from that
light,
from the molten rock that melted my face.
They could not smother that fire.
They could not end the agony of being burned.

Place your fingers beneath your eye
and find the bone that protects it.
Feel its unyielding edge.
Think of rock.
Think of a promontory weathering storms.
My hands. O! my hands could not halt the excavation
that left a crater in my face.
But other hands could.
Last month in Amman,
Iraqi doctors rebuilt the bone structure in my eye socket
in preparation for a prosthetic eye.
And yesterday, in a surgery arranged by Iraqis
and paid for by Americans,

Jordanian doctors restored my sight,
reunited my hands and my one remaining eye.

What my hands alone could not do,
other hands accomplished:
human fingers and palms extinguished the flames of war
and reignited a dark star.

I'll Say It

Amman, Jordan
April, 2008

Um Daoud speaks

I'll say it:
they took him
as you'd take an animal from a yard
and slam it onto a truck
and transport it to a butcher.

They took my first born.

They took Daoud's sixteen-year-old body
like a piece of meat
prime cut,
the child of a goldsmith
and hung it by a hock from a hook in the ceiling.

Dangling there
what could he do but scream
when the electrical prod burned him like a brand,
when its five hundred fingers invaded his body
and turned his muscles to water,
when afterward he hung, twitching?

And what could we do
here at home
when the cupped hands of our cell phone
captured and released
the frantic birds of his terrified voice?

And after we'd given them everything
and fled with Daoud to Jordan,
what could we do when they kidnapped our cousin
and demanded more?

What could we do when they delivered his dismembered body
in a bag to the door of our home in Baghdad?

In your country,
what nightmare form does terror take
when it stalks your dreams?
What animal or mechanical or arthropod shape?

In Iraq, terror takes a human form.
And it walks unmasked under the sun.

I'll say it:
your government took our oil
and left us terror in its place—
a knife at our children's throats,
death at our doorstep.

Break the Lock

Amman, Jordan
May, 2008

Hiwa speaks

The Americans did not tell us they planned to stay.

They did not tell us they came to build a stadium
to brandish their strength,
an arena where helicopters circle and swoop like prehistoric birds of
prey,
where triceratops tanks trample our cities,
where warplanes like weather systems hurl lightning from Iraq's blue
skies.
We stiffened as they flung open the doors to our country and a
steady flow of Western architects, builders, and machinery entered.

They did not tell us they planned to invite terrorists
into this arena,
that Iraq would be a staging ground for apocalyptic combat,
on every side the high ideals of honor and sacrifice fueling the battle,
turning our soil red.

Eleven months later, in early 2004,
waiting in a day labor line at our market in Kirkuk,
we blew on our hands and rocked in our shoes
to keep warm in pre-dawn darkness.
The man who hired us that day
did not tell us we were to work at a US military base in Tikrit.
Ten hours later, en route home, the car that eased in front of our van
did not signal it was wired with explosives.

Leaning over me like a thief
in the molten wreckage,
even the fire lied,
even flames licking my face and torso lied to me.

Whispering comforting words in my ears,
they lulled me into a coma.
But fifteen days later,
I awoke like a newborn rubbed raw, screaming.
And like a newborn, helpless, dependent, I went home.

My wife and children hid every mirror in our house.
They would not tell me my face was a charred field,
a sterile moonscape.
Only the scars forming on my arms and hands and chest spoke the
truth.
Only these scars and a mirror I found a year later in a
        locked cabinet
when my family left me alone in our house.
I did not tell them I knew their secret,
but O! why had I lived to see this day?
Was it to have my wife leave me,
my children turn their back on me and walk away?

Four years later in Iraq, American helicopters still wheel
        and swoop,
and snaking through our cities, military convoys hiss and rattle their
tails.
Their fangs are visible,
but Iraqis are forgotten, locked in a cabinet, hidden like a secret.
How many of us are incognito, unrecognizable?
How many are defaced or have severed limbs,
like broken statuary in a ruined garden?
How many of us wear a map of our country on our face,
        our body?
If my face must be a mirror of Iraq,
then break the lock
and bring it out of the cabinet.
Let Americans see me,
my shriveled nose and ears where cartilage burned,

how my skin contracted as it heated.
Let American fingers touch my scars.
Let Americans befriend me.
Send their weaponry away,
but let American hands help heal me.

Hanan Opened Her Eyes

Amman, Jordan
July, 2008

for Najlaa

Hanan opened her eyes
and saw in the mirror her ripe, olive eyes looking back at her.
She saw burnt and scarred skin on her face,
where the dragon named war breathed on her
and tufts of hair growing in odd patches on her
      scorched scalp.
She saw a deformed and shriveled right ear.

Three years earlier when she was eight years old,
a bomb exploded at a holy site in Najaf,
and Hanan's parents, her three sisters,
and her three brothers
closed their eyes
forever.

We were very close to the building where the bomb exploded.
All I remember is a loud noise and nothing else.

No one expected her to live.

Hanan opened her eyes
and saw a surgeon.
She saw flowers bloom at the tips of his fingers.
She saw fish leap and sparkle in his eyes.

I wish to finish all the operations
and get back my beautiful face
and return to my school and friends.
I want to play with my friends without hearing the words,
"Look at that burnt girl,"
which hurt me so much that I stopped playing.

I need to feel that people accept me when they look at me,
like before.

Hanan closed her eyes during surgery
to separate her thumb and forefinger
where the dragon had welded them together.

She opened them later in the hospital
and looked at the other children on her ward,
some as young as two or three or four years old,
their broken bodies, their missing limbs and eyes, their tears,
their lacerated faces.

She saw them.
She saw playful dolphins plowing seas.
She saw brown pelicans soaring above, plunging into waters.
She held them in her burnt arms,
and they stopped crying.
She offered them a burnt hand,
and they played together.
When she visited the hospital,
when she came to their bedside,
they smiled.
When they looked into Hanan's eyes,
they saw marine mammals leaping,
birds skimming the sea.

Hanan closed her eyes and dreamed.

After a while, she opened her eyes.
She had grown a new mouth, a blowhole, a tail, fins,
a perfect, new skin,
a body sculpted for leaping and diving.
She swam off with her friends.

I Am Here

Rasul in Saint Louis, MO after surgery
August, 2008

for Lori and Kathy C.

I
Even before the bullet,
I was waiting.

Waiting for my window to open on a new world,
for the gray, warring streets to turn green
and Baghdad's gun barrels to become songbirds.
Waiting for sidewalks to repair themselves,
for soccer balls to appear,
for schools to blossom like gardens with children,
with laughter, with learning.

Waiting for our barren world to bear fruit,
waiting for rain to return it to a lump of liquid clay
and my hands to sprout sculptor's fingers
so I could refashion it.

O! the visions I had
locked in our home, listening to gunfire,
bomb blasts,
condemned time dragging its ball and chain.
O, irreconcilable world!

II
The hand that held that gun,
the tendon and muscle that flexed that finger
were not waiting for me,

but I am waiting.

The bullet that pierced my eight-year-old face like a tooth,

the bullet that swallowed one eye
and tore open the other,
the bullet that buried me
was not waiting for me,

but I am waiting.

I am waiting for light like a rescue worker to reach me.
Can you hear light?
Every day I hear its feet.
Every day its voice and its fingers come closer.
I have heard it above me
excavating like rubble the scar tissue on my iris.
I have heard it trying to dissolve the blood clots blocking my sight.

The luminescent hand of the surgeon
is trying to find me at the bottom of this hole
and pull me out,
like my birth,
when the hand of my mother's midwife
drew me out of darkness.
And for the first time light,
like a paintbrush,
began to teach me: color, shadow, depth,
the shape of my mother's face
and the language it speaks,
the unbroken authority and unimpeachable tenderness
in her dark, brown eyes.

Waiting, yes,
and calling: *I am here!*

You Don't Know What Terror Is

Baghdad, Iraq
September, 2008

Karima speaks

You don't know what terror is
until the earth that bore you liquefies,
until your house rocks on wind-whipped waves
and water seeps through its floorboards,
until you are forced to grow gills.

You don't know what terror is
until their fishing boats come trolling down your street,
creeping, monstrous shadows,
their black hulls blotting out the light.

You don't know what terror is
until they hurl their huge nets,
until the world is roped and barred,
until your son is caught
and half-fish, half-man,
not yet knowing who he is
but knowing the world is dangerous, deadly,
he is thrown in the hold,
clubbed,
and forced to sign a confession.

When they bring him to court,
will he be tried as a fish
with the false and crumbling ledge of legal protections
that extends to all marine life
or as a person, coming of age in a time of war,
a boy raised by a widow,
a man tested only on the battlefield?

Thank God There Is Light

Amman, Jordan
September, 2008

for the Direct Aid Iraq team

I

At work, the sniper rarely speaks.
He imagines himself a shadow,
silent, adroit, insubstantial,
a creature withdrawing into cracks and corners,
alone with its thoughts,
murmuring to itself.
He thinks of himself as a negative quality.
His very existence implies an imbalance,
and the will to counter it, to compensate for it,
flows from a natural law that governs his actions.

II

The former Iraqi Army general drives through the city of his birth
and thinks only about the present.
Moving through time in Iraq, he knows,
is like driving through Baghdad,
uncertain, spring-loaded.
We slip from shadow to shadow.
But who can say when a trap will spring
or where?

III

Fed by the sniper's blood,
oxygenated by his inspiration,
pulsing in rhythm with his heart,
the bullet lies, taut and trembling,
in the rifle's cold, metal womb,
an embryo about to be born,
an extension of the sniper's hand,

a claw,
a flat, steel-fisted hammer.

IV
The past is inescapable.
One step behind or just around the corner,
it lies in ambush,
it looks down from rooftops
and leaps.
It recedes and gathers itself rising like a tsunami, a swollen river,
threatening to swamp the present,
flood the future.

V
Launched, the bullet spins out of the gun barrel,
tears through air, and wraps itself in sunlight.
No, it draws the sunlight to itself.
Like a mouth,
like a black hole, it swallows the light.

VI
Amil sits in the car alongside her husband, the former Iraqi Army
general.
Like a metal net thrown on the city,
heavy traffic brings them to a standstill.
She shifts in her seat
and silently curses the traffic
that will make her late for work.
Amil squints in the sunlight.

VII
The bullet has no illusions.
Like most munitions,
it has one short life.
To make the most of it
before penetrating Amil's face,

it shatters the windshield
and with its final breath
blows coarse, glass shards into her eyes,
embedding them in her retina.

VIII
Amil awakes in Amman from a dream of sunlight glinting on water.
She wakes from a dream of eyes,
a dream of Ali,
her sixteen-year-old son
standing in the kitchen, smiling at her.
She wakes from a dream of books
and grimaces.
Amil the reader,
Amil the researcher
hasn't held a book,
hasn't picked up a newspaper
in over a year
since the bullet drove the family from Baghdad to Jordan.

IX
A turgid part of her past rolling over the present like a wave,
the sniper and his bullet are not surprising,
not altogether unexpected.

But Najlaa is unexpected.
Who can account for Najlaa
advocating and arranging health care for Iraqis—
a refugee herself, her own family torn and scattered—
who can account for her standing firm in Amman
like high ground,
like a rock to cling to
to build on
while waters rise?
And Rana and Yasir and Dr. Mazen and Dr. Ghada, her Iraqi colleagues?

And the ordinary, nameless Americans sharing their money and concern?
Nothing in Amil's past to suggest their existence,
nothing to suggest their offering to pay
for surgery to restore her sight.

X
Amil awakes after surgery, sleeps,
wakes, sleeps again.
A nurse removes her bandages.
She opens her eyes and looks at Najlaa.
Thank God there is light, Amil says
and smiles.
She reaches for a newspaper.
She holds it in front of her eyes
and reads.

Home at the Al-Monzer Hotel

Amman, Jordan
October, 2008

for Mazen, Abdul-Azeem, Hamdi, Omar

Lies pursued us.
Like waves during a storm, they hammered and eroded our humanity,
like an undertow, threatened to drag us down and out, drown us.

The lie of consumerism.
The lie of big houses.
The lie of upward mobility, free markets . . .
The lie of patriotism and its war on friendship.

A hurricane assault on our spirit
hurled us out to sea.

We came to the Al-Monzer Hotel like castaways, like pilgrims,
wind-whipped, waterlogged, hungry.
Your bottomless smiles, like beacons, guided us to shore.
You greeted us with hot soup and hospitality,
stories of rare birds who stop at your inn,
and over the subsequent days and weeks,
beneath answers to a hundred questions and endless translations,
behind assistance with the mobile phone settings and repairs,
an unmistakable joy in our company,
an unforgettable solicitude.
In short, in a word,
though our government forbids it,
friendship.
And friendship, with its long arms, wrapped us,
a barrier reef or wetland,
a haven,
home.

Artists without Chains

Baghdad, Iraq
October, 2008
third annual Week of Nonviolence

In the silence between bomb blasts,
you conceived your words, embryos in your artists' minds,
and fed them with your blood,
where they stirred and kicked to be born,
though not yet, not yet,
for who would choose to raise children in a battlefield?

But art demands to speak in its native time and place,
and so your words were born
in Baghdad,
under bombardment,
Baghdad under curfew,
Baghdad in the thundering nightmare of war.

Bloody and breathing,
naked as a heart, as a lung,
veined and vulnerable,
they lay in your arms.

With paintbrush and crayon and chalk,
with pen and ink and charcoal,
you clothed them in feathers,
you anointed them with light,
framed them with thin and hollow bones for flying
and, in the public square
under a blue, expansive sky
into the welcoming warmth of an October sun,
you released them.

In the city of security barriers and military checkpoints,

they fly without impediment.
On the city of weeping parents and orphaned children,
on the city of flaming cars and mangled buildings,
they land like a kiss.

You let them loose in the world.

They reach us even here.

The Education of Iraq's Children

Iraq
October, 2008

In Iraq, thanks to America and its military,
our children are multilingual.
In addition to Arabic and Kurdish, our national languages,
they are fluent in war and its two primary linguistic branches,
terror and displacement.

By the time Iraqi children are two,
they know every letter in the alphabet of fear
and recognize dozens of words in the lexicon of hunger.
They understand the consonant vocalization of boots kicking in a
door,
the vowel sounds of missiles wailing, parents weeping, other children
screaming,
the sly connotations of checkpoints and barbed wire and blast walls.
They assimilate war's unspoken assumptions, its philosophical declara-
tions,
its phonetic ordinances.

Its grammar and semantics encompass them, an atmosphere
where the sun shines, rain falls, wind blows.
Inhaled into their lungs,
words of war travel their bloodstream,
touching every cell in every child's body,
every neuron in the developing mind
of Iraq's embryonic future.

Geese Fly Over Basra

Basra, Iraq
October, 2008

Um Heyder and Um Ali speak

At first, we simply heard them.
The sound of their trajectory
reaching us from thousands of feet above.
A foreign tongue, yes,
but like doumbek, like lute
primordial, native,
a chorus of voices singing
their universal language of longing.

At that height
in that blue light,
all things are absorbed, scattered.
We could not find them.
And still their voices came to us,
called us, sang,

and our own hearts leapt
into the blue,
into the buoyant, blue void.
And we, too, flew,
we, too, rode across that remote and wind-swept lake
leaning on our luck,
a song in our throats,
the powerful arms of our own longing beating the
        blue, thin air.

A Welcome Word

Baghdad, Iraq
October, 2008

Fifteen-year-old Mahdi Mohammad speaks

I
A year ago today,
my mother handed me money
and sent me to the market.
We have no bread, she said.
I remember that moment before I left the house
as if it were a holiday, wholeness, happiness itself.
I carry it with me like a photo, like a limb.

At the market,
a bomb waited for me like a thief, like a gang.
It opened its gaping mouth and roared.
Breaking my jaw, its eight fists beat my face.
Ruining my eye, its eighty claws raked me.

In Baghdad, bombs not bread.

II
What is an eye?
If it is a door, then a glass one.
If a lens, then mine is shuttered.
If a window, then shattered.

What is a bomb?
I say a mouth
swallowing people whole.
A clawed hand
gouging hospitals, schools, mosques.
A fist

punching its way through glass,
weighing the air with shards
that lodge in peoples' lungs,
litter the streets.

Who can say what a face is?
I cannot,
but take away its eye,
and it is broken.

Break your finger,
and it will heal.
But break a window,
and it is broken.
Break your face,
and you are maimed, a mutant, a monster, a nightmare.

At school, mockery broke my will,
drove me out of the classroom,
off the playground,
into the street.

III
In Baghdad, there are eyes on our streets.
They stare up at me as I walk.
Mindless as marbles, they stare at walls, trees, sky.
The eyes of Iraqi children litter our streets.
People turn their heads, avert their eyes,
dam the river of their grief.

IV
A word cannot heal my face.
But last week a welcome word reached us.
It took almost a year to arrive,
a promise sailing to us from America,

crossing, on foot, the Syrian Desert from Jordan.
It brought an invitation:
Come to Amman, where a doctor will replace your eye,
restore your humanity.

I carry these words in my pocket wherever I go.

The Eyes of These Two Children

from Ukiah, California
October, 2008

for bg

October and Mill Creek, torrential after winter rains,
is a trickle, a testament to tenacious ice and snow
still clinging to rock and shade in mountains.
All summer and into autumn, thin fingers of water roll and sift sand,
turning particles over and over,
a mind intent on its thoughts,
pondering questions.

If questions can lead us
like a star or signpost,
if questions can steer us like a lodestone,
let this be one: how can we be
responsible to Iraqis
ten thousand miles away,
caught in the teeth of war?

Be strong, be smart, and stay with us, Haider says,
for the whole world has forgotten us.

If a question can draw us like a horizon or a mountain pass,
if a question can become a quest,

if a question can accompany us,
if, like a partner, it can settle into our soul,
if, like an embryo, it can take root and grow,
let it be this one:
How can I enact a commitment to Iraqi people?

I carry these thoughts while walking among oak trees
on a leafy animal trail above Mill Creek,
a path where people and animals have always walked,

a place where the very idea of always could have been conceived.
Daily, I gather acorns for food
and study deer, squirrels, birds, and bear
who also gather these glossy, plump, pointed gifts,
who uncover, beneath the leaf duff of my mind, memories and questions.
I move among other presences
and a thousand generations of hunter-gatherers accompany me.
Time stretches backward and forward,
and my connection to people follows.
Released from the corral of rational thought,
my mind embraces connections with other species
and with people across the globe.
Experience is its own certification.
I dwell, like all creatures, in a vast, complex kaleidoscope
of time and space.

In this context, I consider an event in Iraq.
Last week, in Karrada, a usual convoy
of SUVs and armored security guards—
usual, that is, if you watch Fox News
or if you are a child growing up in Baghdad,
questioning it, turning it over and over,
reading it with the deft fingers of your mind,
fingering the familiar physiognomy of your world
and finding it comprised of barbed wire, broken bones,
burnt out and bullet-ridden cars.
The convoy was usual, too, in its deadliness, its taut and
explicit threat,
like unexploded ordnance: Come too close and I will maim you.
And an all-too-usual outcome:
a car failed to perceive the threat,
broke an invisible line, triggered a barrage of bullets,
and two women lay shattered and dead in its front seat.

Corporate officials offered an initial assessment:

Our security team was approached at speed
by a vehicle that failed to stop
despite an escalation of warnings.
Finally shots were fired at the vehicle and it stopped.

The statement failed to mention the two adult hearts that also
stopped
and the heart failure of guards who fled
without securing medical aid for the injured.
Eye witnesses testified they raced off like gangsters.
It also failed to account for two children in the back seat,
their racing hearts failing for the moment
to comprehend the meaning of blood and brains and hair
spattering the upholstery inside the car and their clothes—
and stuck to windows.

Despite the legerdemain of denial,
other statements made clear the nature of questions that turn
in the minds of US officials
and that waging war is one part weaponry,
three parts public relations.

State Department spokesman Sean McCormack said the shooting
had *nothing to do with the State Department or the US government.*

In like form, a US embassy spokeswoman in Baghdad
said the shooting was not connected with the embassy
and *that USAID does not direct the security arrangements of [its] con-*
tractors.

If a question can lead us, try these:
What part of a child is amputated
when her parent or relative is killed in front of her?
When she wakes after surgery,
where is the pain centered,
where are the bandages laid,

where does the wound ooze, the scar form?

Fingering the deep soils of our minds,
let us search for the sharpest and most tender words
and fit them onto the arrows of sentences.
Let us notch them to the bowstring of paragraphs
and, aiming at the architects of this war,
release them.

Let us become the words that we embrace
and let us walk, voluble, into their offices,
forbidding them to hide for another moment
from the eyes of these two children.

Najlaa

Amman, Jordan
November, 2008

Najlaa, you enter our lives like laughter,
like music,
like fire,
like drumbeat at dawn in a forest.
You feed us.
We are changed forever.

You enter our day like morning,
like a star stepping above a horizon, summiting a mountain,
like a river of light.

Light massages our war-weary minds.

Light touches the earth and bulbs sprout.
Flowers bud, trees leaf, birds sing at your approach,
and in these war-darkened times,
when compassion is so out of fashion,
love leads us forward,
love lights our way.

We Remember

Iraq
November, 2008

Iraqi mothers speak

We remember our children,
each of them as a single grain of sand in the oyster shell of our
wombs,
how for nine months we coated them with nacre
and the perfect gems we birthed—
Hind, Haider, Rami, Hanan.

We remember.

We remember and we see the black boot of sanctions and war
and occupation,
its print everywhere in our country,
how it tramples our most precious treasures,
how it breaks our children,
cracks, shatters, and crushes their round, shining bodies:
our pearls seized and thrown before marauding swine.

Only His Eyes

Amman, Jordan
November, 2008

Nabil's father speaks

Nabil. Nabil. Nabil.

As though explosions and the compressed rage they release
were all shoulders and arms and fingers,
the car bomb reached across the street,
heaved Nabil off the ground,
and threw him on his head.

Nabil. Nabil. Nabil.

Terrified, the boy stood, stumbled, ran home.

For two weeks, no one knew the bomb clung to him,
no one could see the bomb still held him.

But its anger not yet spent,
the bomb erupted again,
shook Nabil so that he lost his balance.
It squeezed his throat and garbled his words.
It cast a shadow across his mind, ruined his memory,
invaded his body, and loosened his bladder and bowels.

Out of iron rage, the bomb built a cage,
out of stony brutality, a prison his father cannot enter,
out of molten anger, it cast a lock his father's voice cannot pick.

Nabil. Nabil. Nabil.
Only the boy's eyes,

only his eyes offer a way into the past,
a way to reach, a way back to

Nabil.

*from an interview conducted by Sama Alshaibi and
Najlaa Al-Nashi*

Welcome

Abu Abbas' kitchen in Amman, Jordan
January, 2009

*I'm going to make you a famous Iraqi dish,
and God willing, when it is finished, you will like it,* Abu Abbas said,
slamming the chicken down on the cutting board
and deftly quartering it.

Sometimes violence is a lightning strike,
sudden, explosive, external.
We have this in Iraq, he said.
And people try to stay inside, out of the weather.

But violence can also spread as a disease.
Where is safety when your neighborhood is infected?
When a militia targets you,
there are no holes in the sky
that you can climb through into another world,
no magic to make wings sprout from your back
and a zippered pouch appear in front for your children,
no moonlit doorway into tree or mountain.

In Baghdad, Abu Abbas recounted,
*eighteen to twenty young men, armed, in cars
came onto our street.
They killed my neighbor.
They followed him to his house,
and poor guy, he tried to run away
but they got him.
He lay there on the street in front of us, dying,
but anyone who helped him would be dead.
His children were screaming for us to do something.*

We were ashamed because we are grown men,
but they told us,
"Anyone who helps will be shot."
He stabbed the paring knife downward for emphasis.
Imagine this situation.
Your friend, your brother, your sister cries for help.
They are right in front of you, and you have a car,
but you are forbidden to help.
There is no country in the world
where this situation is acceptable.

In the cramped kitchen,
steam condensed on the ceiling and windows and walls.
Dented, aluminum lids rattled on pots.
Abu Abbas wiped the sweat from his forehead.

The next day they called me and said,
"Cooperate with us or you are next."
I was scared because I have five young children.
Remember, they had just killed my neighbor
in front of my eyes.
They wanted me to share in their crimes,
to identify who is Sunni and who is Shia, he explained,
patting the air, shaping it like dough.
I was welcome in every home in the neighborhood, he continued,
so I could do this.

Abu Abbas turned and took a breath.
He stepped across the kitchen and placed a hand over the burner,
checking the heat.
Turning back, he said,
I hid at my brother's home,
but the militia called.
"We know where you are," they said,
and, of course, they did.
They have eyes everywhere.

What do you want from me, I asked?
"Meet with us," they said,
"and we will tell you."
But I knew what they would say.
They would offer to protect my family and me
in exchange for information.
If I went,
I would be dipping my hands in their blood.

His family stood at the edge of a precipice,
water spilling over rocks,
water leaping into a void
and landing in a frenzied pool below.
The roar rattled Abu Abbas.

I was shocked and afraid.
I tried to imagine myself a drop of water in that stream.
My mind froze.
Impossible, I thought,
but we couldn't turn back upstream
and work with the militia.
Me do that? Impossible.

On the stove, water boiled, rice steamed.

I went home, and that same day we decided to leave.
Early, early in the morning.
I said the Shahada and prayed two recitations,
because I was sure I was going to die.
We took nothing with us,
but we weren't coming back.
Walking out of my house, I didn't look.
I thought I would be killed right there, Abu Abbas said,
puncturing the air with the knife in his hand,
and my wife and children would be crying over me.

The impossible journey from Baghdad

to the border with Jordan
took an entire day.
We left the house at six in the morning,
got on a bus,
and arrived at dawn the next day.

They called me on my cell phone when we were traveling.
"Where are you?" they asked.
I told them: at the market.
"Meet with us," they demanded.
OK, I said, I am on my way.
I will meet you in half an hour.
And I turned off my phone.

But the border itself is a locked gate
with armed guards,
a sieve screening out unwanted immigrants.

They weren't taking men, thirty-five years old or younger.
And I was thirty-five.
"Are you refugees?" the border official asked.
I don't know, I said, but we come to you by the grace of God.
We can't go back.
I told him our story.

"You can enter," he said. "And we welcome you."

For centuries in southern Iraq, Bedouin farmers and shepherds made their livelihood from land and water. In the wake of the invasion, however, laws that regulated water usage have crumbled, and people upstream have diverted and drained the river. By the time it reaches their fields, it is a trickle, a bony finger, incapable of providing sustenance. Young Bedouin men are leaving their homes for the cities, leaving their country for Jordan and Syria, seeking a way to support their families. Adil is one of these young men.

A Time When

Amman, Jordan
January, 2009

Adil speaks

In Al-Muthanna, Iraq,
rocks watch,
sands listen.
Wind roams widely, gathering
in its ten thousand hands
sounds, syllables, words, voices.

The land has a long memory.
It recalls a time
before the US invasion
when water was a birthright,
when this river near our home flowed uninterrupted,
a blue needle knitting,
a liquid shuttle weaving
time,
threading past and future
in one living tapestry.

A time not long ago
when Bedouin fathers and sons woke to work their fields,
came home to hold children in their arms,
when sheep clothed and fed us,

when rice signed its name on the earth in green ink,
our family alone producing seven tons a year

A time, long ago, when our Bedouin people did not exist

A time,
even,
before war.

She Was Seventeen

Basra, Iraq
March, 2009

Ihsan speaks

In January of 1991,
a time of gathering darkness
when daylight and springtime were prohibited
under an international embargo,
Ruqayya was seventeen,
glowing,
a night lantern,
a winter bloom.

Spring stirred in her—
Mohammad and Ahmed and Zaineb—
seeds housed within her frame,
waiting to sprout, to be born

despite the drought we call sanctions already parching the land.

She was seventeen the month the warplanes came
across the globe from America and Europe,
squadron after squadron,
fleet flocks in formation,
a terrible migration of mechanical raptors
brandishing their uranium-tipped talons and beaks.

The year the US and Great Britain
turned southern Iraq into a hazardous waste site,
a toxic dump,
a threat to anything that moves and breathes and eats.

She was seventeen the month the missiles fell,
an acid, heavy-metal rain,
a uranium rain,

a forty-day, toxic cloud burst,
weaponry soaking our soil,
planting its cancer deep in our land
forever;

the year the bombs invaded her body,
crawling inside her
to launch their time-release, explosive, radioactive egg sacs,
occupying her flesh,
colonizing her future.

She was seventeen.

Tarfiq Did Not Come Here to Die

Amman, Jordan
April, 2009

Risking our ankles picking a way across a ruined, rock-strewn lot,
sidestepping a disemboweled rat something caught
and left to dry in Amman's relentless sun,
a cold wind cracking a sandstone whip, stinging us—
it is easier to arrive.

Easier to step out of radiant April light,
duck through an entrance into the cave of this small, dark apartment,
and shuffle up to this bed where Tarfiq lies,
eyes closed somewhere between rest and waking,
seven hundred fifty miles from home.

Uranium weapons made him sick, Ali says,
Ali who left work and family to accompany his friend.
He is not the first.

Tarfiq did not come here from Basrah to die.

His family sold their home and furniture, Ali says,
to pay for surgery.
Friends loaned him money.

Tarfiq did not come here to lie in the dark
unable to move his left leg,
massaging his useless left arm,
the rhythmic strokes soothing his mind
while thieving cancer, picking and choosing,
robs him of one body part after another.

Your wife and children must be worried about you, I said.

A labored response,

Yes.
A single chord but full, forte
struck with all the breath he can muster.

I have two girls, eight and four, and a six-year-old son . . .

Yes, he likes to play soccer . . . like his father.

In a corner behind the door, leaning against a wall,
an aluminum crutch Tarfiq uses to steady himself
and walk, dragging his unresponsive left leg.

Sadly, a Jordanian oncology lab report reads,
four days post-op, a massive recurrence . . .
We treated it aggressively.

The final question asked and answered,
we sit in dim light, empty-handed,
without a single vital word,
unwilling or unable to leave,
silence separating us,
dropping us deeper within ourselves,
binding us in one body of grief and longing.

In Iraq, we are seeing more and more malignant tumors, especially brain cancer. This is because of the environmental pollution of modern warfare.

—Najlaa Al-Nashi, Iraqi medical researcher

We Did Not Imagine You

Amman, Jordan
April, 2009

We came as far as imagination would carry us:
this small, dark, concrete cell where Tarfiq lies,
cancer a fire in his brain,
short-circuiting its electric, animal intelligence,
separating his spirit from the body it animates.

We did not come to see you, Ali,
a poor factory worker from Basrah,
weary, unshaven, unknown outside this room.
We did not even imagine you, the shoulder Tarfiq leans on,
the arms that carried him from Basrah to Amman,
the hands that make his tea, his coffee, his meals.

I am stunned to learn you left family and work to accompany Tarfiq.

The treatment plan, you explain,
is six weeks of chemo and radiation
followed by six months of chemo.
And still you stand here.

The room spins, the world falls away,
and when my eyes clear, Ali,
there is only you.
I am drawn to you as a plant to light,
hands to warmth,
migrating birds to that latitude and longitude
where life and love are supported.

I want to ask you questions I cannot ask.
I want to know you.

Instead, I say to Tarfiq,
You have a good friend here.

Yes, he says,
the effort of lifting his head to speak costing him,
a single, pained syllable substituting for every gesture, every
     story,
every word he might have spoken.

If Irony Were Justice

Amman, Jordan
May, 2007

Somewhere, Mustafa knows, he has a twin brother,
an American soldier with wheels for legs,
a man who stands for nothing,
a man who is no longer a man
who urinates through a tube into a bag,
an American digging into the bureaucratic rubble of his government
trying to unearth something human,
trying to locate a surgeon's fingers to reset the clock of his life
and point him forward.

If irony were iron,
Mustafa's back would have held
when four years ago today
the force of a US missile swept him like a branch from his roof
and dropped him two stories below in his garden.

If irony were bread,
a small round of dough, pounded, stretched, flattened,
and thrown on a fire,
a bowl of hummus dribbled with olive oil,
a cool yogurt and cucumber salad,
Mustafa would never be hungry here in Amman.

For three years he rolled his chair through Baghdad—
one more broken body bent to its wheel—
and along concrete and barbed wire barriers that line the Green
Zone
seeking reparation for his injuries.

I left no door unknocked, he says.

If irony were justice,

the US military would have given him more than a letter:

Mustafa Samir Hassan was injured
when a missile exploded near his home
in the Karrada neighborhood of Baghdad on April 3rd, 2003.

It would instead have given him:
anesthesia, scalpels, transfusions, trained fingers, aftercare.

Somewhere, Mustafa knows, there is a clinic
with doctors who can repair his back,
who can reorient his life toward the future.
But for now, he is still trying to learn about this war from his television,
still climbing a ladder to fix an antenna on his house in Baghdad,
still falling
like a long-stemmed glass
to hard ground.

Originally pubished in *Battlefield without Borders*, David Smith-Ferri,
Haley's, First Printing, 2007; Second Printing, 2008

Like Love Itself

Amman, Jordan
April, 2009

Um Mustafa speaks

I
When you have nothing,
some choices are simpler, clearer.

Don't marvel at my traveling alone across the desert—
Amman a distant star, a prisoner's waking dream—
or my facing criminal customs officials
who would sell your life to a militia for a hundred dollars.
I know the value of my life
and who owns it.
I also know the stories
of people turned away at the border for no reason.
All the criminals need is a discreet phone call describing
your clothes and transport,
and another Iraqi is robbed and beaten and left to die.
No Samaritans walk that road.

II
I arrived in Amman unexpected
like a telegram, like love itself,
and found my son, Mustafa,
five years after the US missile had found him,
five years after its hot, hurricane breath had blown him
off the second story roof of his Baghdad home
and broken his back.
It felt like the air kicked me, he told us.

What do American missile makers know about their weapons?
In their labs, in their factories, what are they thinking?
Were they thinking about my son's legs when they
        built their missile?

When they packed it with knives, did they know it would cut Musta-
fa's vertebrae, separate his brain from his legs?
Do they know now that his brain has lost his legs,
that it searches like a bereaved mother but cannot find anything be-
low his waist?

A missile casts a long shadow.
In Baghdad, Mustafa could not escape it.
Hope, like a sunflower, like a lily locked in a closet,
withered, fell.
He was twenty-three years old
and already mourning his youth.

III
But in Amman, I filled my hands with Mustafa.
I held his arm, touched his face, laid my hand on his shoulder.
Like a blind person, my fingers sprouted eyes.
I stored memories in my hands to carry back to Baghdad.

When you have nothing to hold,
your hands become doorways, rivers, philosophers, tongues.
They spoke my love, my longing,
my grief,
my memory of the past,
my vision of a new life.

IV
Missiles can leave large craters,
wide, uncrossable chasms.
They can also cause a conflagration.
Health care, running before the flames, has fled Iraq.
In Baghdad, Mustafa found himself in a wheelchair
at the bottom of a hole
and no hands, no rope to help him.

But in Amman, I found Mustafa above ground,
supple, springtime, leafing out, green.
O, in Amman something new.
People separated by more than oceans and continents,
more than language and culture,
hand in hand now, working together.
People separated by fire and craters,
by missiles and bullets and the lies that fire them,
working together,
making of their linked arms and hands
a rope, a basket, a way up and out.
Americans and Iraqis side by side.
Mustafa—
crippled by a US missile,
ignored by the US government,
left to rot in an open grave—
befriended,
offered hands, hospitality, health care.

I knew that Americans weren't evil,
and now I have proof.

Thresholds

Amman, Jordan
April, 2009

Like children crowding together at the edge of a bluff,
a sea swirling below,
we gather at the top of the stairwell
while first Yasir and then Noah climb down
and wade into Amman's fading twilight.
Returning, they half push, half carry Mustafa and his
wheelchair
up from those depths,
across the threshold and into the apartment.
A foaming, salt-water joy washes over us.

Dinner can wait.

We watch amazed as Mustafa
without assistance
heaves himself up from the vinyl and metal hole of his wheelchair
and dripping with pleasure
stands eye-to-eye among us.

Leaning now on a walker,
shifting his weight back and forth, back and forth
and willing the hard-to-reach muscles in his right thigh to move that
leg,
he articulates how long the road to adulthood is
and how far he has come
in teaching his body to stand, to balance,
how close he is, at twenty-nine years,
to learning to walk again.

Across the room,

five-month-old Ammar is propped with pillows
and sitting on a couch practicing, practicing—
learning to move his hands, his arms,
heaving his body left and right,
leaning, over-leaning, catching his balance.

Ammar records every labored move the older man makes,
reacts to every salty smile that washes over him,
follows the arc of every spark that leaps from Mustafa's brown, Iraqi
eyes.

Voices of Young, Single Iraqi Men

Amman, Jordan
April, 2009

Before we visited Tarfiq and Ali,
before Ghada and I stepped off the bank into that
    liminal place
between river and sea
into brackish water,
sound of breakers ahead
and beyond that, eternity of ocean and uncharted horizon;

before we bid Tarfiq farewell,
adding one final flower to his small craft,
the current tugging,
the frayed rope tether soon to snap,
we entered a crumbling stairwell
and, accompanied by the smell of urine,
climbed three flights and disappeared.

A journey of only a few minutes on foot
but as though we'd climbed into mountains themselves,
terrain steep, remote, rugged,
water white and fast
careening through narrow clefts in rock,
threatening to sweep the banks,
thundering through gorges,
the constant roar itself dominating, godlike, indivisible.

And there, in that thin air,
in that alpine land of snowmelt and headwaters,
the young men of Iraq
disappeared, erased,
forgotten among boulders,
crouched in canyons:
Haithim and Hadi and Nasir.

Under Saddam,
you had to be in the Ba'ath Party.

In Iraq, I was a cadet training for the Fida'in Saddam,
the army's special youth guard.
After the invasion, the militias came after us.
I saw many killed.

In Basra, the Badr Brigade burned our house
and beat my mother.
They shot my brother.
When I saw him in a wheelchair,
I tried to fight back.
Now they want me.

Adel and Ahmed,
forgotten, invisible,
battered against rocks:

Here in Jordan, people are afraid of us,
afraid of young, single men.
They avoid us.
No one thinks of our situation.

No country will accept us.
If UNHCR would tell us there is no hope, then OK.
Instead, they tell us nothing.
"Your case," they say, "is under study."

I have an infection in my liver and lungs.
I spent fifteen days in the hospital,
but I can't afford medication.
No one covers aftercare.

Life for us in Jordan is no different than in Iraq.
How can I tell you?

In Iraq, they put your eyes out
and cut off your hands.
Here, they tie your arms
and throw salt in your face.
Tell me the difference.
I didn't die in Iraq like others,
but life here is a death, too.

Hussein and Assad
living in that river:

I came here five years ago,
when I was fourteen.

They killed my father.
Now I am the oldest.

My father is in a wheelchair.
I came here to find work
and support our family.

It is illegal for us to work here,
and the police are watching, listening,
hunting us.
If they catch you,
it is back to Iraq.
It happens every day.
And what then?

Odaij and Muaed
clinging to slippery rocks:

We are five people in my family,
in five different countries now.

Here in Jordan I was arrested at work
and put in prison.
But I was lucky.
My employer paid a bribe.
A lot of people are not so lucky.

The river's thousand arms batter
while its infinite fingers pummel
and pull.

We Know

Amman, Jordan
April, 2009

Even as sky darkens and clouds gather
even as air hums

Even as lightning images flash
and memories rumble and crack above us

Even as Abu Hassan's words, the first fat drops, fall

    torture   *Abu Ghraib*   *prisoners killing each other*

Even after an hour, with his narrative swirling at our feet
threatening to drag us downstream,
we know this is not the story he wants to tell.

Even as he leans toward us, eyes looking directly into ours—

even as he sits in front of us, intact,
we know that his survival isn't the real story.

As Um Hassan says,
While my husband was in prison, we managed.
But it was very difficult for the children to lose their father,
and it was becoming dangerous at school ...

As Abu Hassan says,
Just because I was refused resettlement,
just because they took my life away in Iraq
doesn't mean my children must remain like prisoners here in Jordan.

We know this story isn't about the past,
but the future,

not about the father,
but the children.

This is Not Old News

Amman, Jordan
April, 2009

for Dr. Ghada

Under a sky so light and remote it threatens to drift away
and abandon these homes,
we follow Abu Hassan wordlessly
up yet another shattered walk,
deeper into another anonymous neighborhood,
past feral cats who pick through garbage
and draw silently into shadows or behind walls
waiting for us to pass.

This is where the invisible live,
the faceless and voiceless, the nameless.
People without papers.
People without a present or future.
The people with only a past.

And so our conversation leaps backward five and a half years
into a time when Iraq still existed
in the months after the American invasion.

I lived in a dangerous place, Abu Hassan begins
with characteristic understatement,
a small farm on fertile land ringing Fallujah.
Chickens, a cow, tomatoes, cucumbers, fruit trees.
We didn't ask for war,
and when it came, we couldn't escape its jaws.

One night, he says, stepping into that time, that place
and drawing us in after him,

an exchange of gunfire from the direction of my neighbor's farm.
I heard it, but did I know who held the guns, who pulled the triggers?
Did I know what was in their hearts?

Two hours later without knocking, war entered Abu Hassan's home.
Teeth bared, barking orders,
every muscle taut and electric with battle,
US Marines burst through his door,
separated Abu Hassan from his wife and children,
threw him to the ground,
pointed a gun to the back of his head,
and demanded information about the resistance.

They went through everything, Um Hassan says.
They even checked inside the baby's diapers
and inside the pillows.

Their guns, Abu Hassan adds,
were bigger than our children.
Every day our son lives with memories of that night
and its terror.
Like a heart, it beats inside him,
feeding the dreams which visit him at night.

This is not old news.

The Americans had no evidence, but they took me anyway.

Later, in prison, an interrogator told him,
When we take fire,
if we can't find the assailants,
we'll arrest anyone in the area.
Chances are, we'll get someone who's guilty
or who knows something.

Abu Hassan got a year of imprisonment.
First, seven days at the American camp at Al-Tariq.

They used every kind of torture and abuse.

Detention in another camp in Baghdad
where *the torture was psychological*
and then, beginning mid-January 2004,
five months at Abu Ghraib.

This is the same period when the world is learning
about the abuse there.

But Abu Hassan wasn't held in one of the underground cells
where that abuse occurred—
instead, a terror the world never learned of,
under large tents in an open yard with nearly a thousand other prisoners.

Terrible conditions.
Almost no food,
very cold and little protection against the weather.
And worst,
because the US military was housed there,
daily insurgent mortar attacks on the camp.

As though the prisoners were invisible or simply forgotten,
as though they were dead already
or dying and not worth the trouble,
as though they were so much refuse heaved on a garbage dump,
when shells landed among them, *no protection was provided.*

We were caught in the middle
between the attackers and the US military.
We never knew when a next attack would occur or from where—

and no place to hide.
During my time in detention,
perhaps 120 of us were killed and others, wounded.

Among the Americans, at least one person with eyes and a memory,
with a heart and a willingness to voice its unease.

A young doctor.
A representative from the prisoners went with him
and spoke to the authorities.

The next stop in Abu Hassan's 2004 tour of American detention
centers
was Bucca Camp in Basrah.

Here, conditions were better.
More and better quality food.
And safer.

Safer . . . at first.
But every day,
fundamentalist militants were transferred into Bucca.

Soon Bucca Camp was filled with them and their proselytizing,
their pamphlets and papers and study circles.
Like a disease, they tried to multiply themselves.
I opposed them and their views,
and they beat me with fists and clubs.
Where were the Americans?

We became two groups in the camp,
divided
like our country.
Maybe eight hundred extremists and one hundred non-extremists.
As in Iraq outside our prison,

one group tried to swallow the other.

This is not old news.

They attacked,
killing two of us and wounding twenty-five.
Again, the Americans did nothing to protect us.
Instead, at night, we posted our own guards.

Looking me straight in the eye,
Abu Hassan lets this image linger, quiver,
fade.
Then he continues,

All the suffering of torture and hunger at the previous camp
was nothing compared to these days.
I wished I could go back.

Later, an American interrogator told him,
It's not our problem.

Upon release, upon returning home,
death threats from Al-Qaida members
who recognized him from prison.

I've lost my whole life.
I've been kept in prison.
I have nothing in Iraq now.
I'm forty-one. How can I start over now?
And here in Jordan, I am allowed to exist
but not to live.

This is not old news.

Why We Tell Stories

with Abu Hassan's family
Amman, Jordan
April, 2009

for Rachael and Jessica

Pretending to fashion from dry bones
lives, histories, relationships, people,
the world will argue numbers,
but no matter how you count displaced Iraqis
(by ones and twos, by thousands, by millions),
you cannot total them.

Probably they do not even exist, cynics surmise,
for what is a number anyway?

And whose television screen shows
where Iraqis have fallen on narrow, granite shelves
and remote, rocky ledges?
Who sees them looking for handholds,
risking their limbs, their lives to regain the top,
jagged rocks and an empty-bellied ocean bellowing below?

We can count them away, sinister minds conclude,
count them right off the cliff.

Yes, count them until they are washed out by distance,
pixilated, impressionistic images
indistinguishable from the shadowy rock behind them.

But you cannot count even this one family,
even these three children,
standing in a tiny apartment here in al-Hashmi.
No rope can measure their grief,
no calculus, no geometry,
no container to quantify their loss.

Under a New Sky

Amman, Jordan
April, 2009

Iraqi refugees speak

We came, Selma says,
with only the clothes on our backs,
my three children and I,
in terror, with only the clothes on our backs.

They drove us like dogs
out of our schools, our homes, our cities, our country,
every step of the way stones landing among us.
They took our land, our livestock,
our bedrooms, kitchens, carpets, keepsakes . . .
They locked the gates behind us
and posted armed guards.

I cannot return, Yasir says. *They will kill me.*

They seized the sound of our rivers—
that music that rocks our land to sleep at night,
inspires its dreams,
wakes it at dawn.
With rope and chain,
they bound it in a heavy bag
and threw it into a cave,
piling rocks at the entrance.
They thought they could subdue and break it,
but to this day the hills tremble with its struggles.
They thought they could contain it,
but we carry it with us in our laughter,
in our flutes and pipes and drums,
in our violins and ouds,
in our throats,
in our blood.

We will not forget the rivers
beside which we were born, Mazen says.

They burned our theaters,
bulldozed our playgrounds,
emptied our colleges and universities,
lifting the buildings in their hands
and shaking the students out the windows.
They laughed as we ran,
laughed as we hid in our homes,
curtains drawn, doors locked.
They slit our teachers' throats
and dumped them
like fish heads
in the gutters.
They told us, *You will never be brave.*
You will never again have friends.

They told us, *You are alone.*
They tried to cut each of our branches off its tree.
But our grain is twisted, our wood is iron.
Their blades dulled, their saws smoked and burned.
They tried to make us orphans.
They told us, *You have no family.*
They killed my sisters, your uncles, her parents, his cousins, their children.
So we found each other
in a foreign land,
in a strange city,
in a new year.

And in a wood we'd never known,
we spread blankets,
gathered sticks,
built fires,
brewed tea in old pots.

And under a new sky
we covered the blankets with biryani,
tabouleh, masgouf, dolma,
honey and raisins and almonds,
pistachios and dates.
Cardamom and coriander and tamarind rose in steam from the trays.
And together, under a new sky, we ate.

Afterward, Dorgham and Sirwan lifted their doumbek drums,
unzipped their covers,
pressed them like a child against their hips,
and unlocked their voices.
Tabor sang old songs from Basrah,
and we knew we were all children.
We linked our hands, Tabor at the head of the line,
and in one body,
like a snake,
yes, like a river,
we danced and sang
under a new sky.

Necklace

Amman, Jordan
April, 2009

IIf you wonder where or how or whether
you come into this story,
consider that even the telling of it is a slow and careful sifting
     of words and images
and the retelling a journey of many nights through uncharted land.
Consider that the story doesn't exist apart from the people
     who lived it,
that words themselves are flesh and bone and blood
groping for contact,
precious links that the storyteller fashions into an unbreakable
     necklace
and that hearing, itself, is the deliberate practice
     of wearing that fine, hand-crafted art.

II
In the cramped apartment in Amman,
Abu Ammar looked at his hands
open in front of him
as at the illustrated leaves of a book
and saw all the jewelry they had made and sold
and given as gifts,
three decades of gold and turquoise, craft and commerce.

He turned back to a late-May morning in 1999,
the sun pouring its rivers through the windows
of his storefront goldsmith shop.
Holding the fine-spun threads of a gold necklace in
     front of him,
he admired not only the way they gathered and transmitted light
but also their feigned delicacy, their subtle resilience.

He knew they would both signal abiding strength
and circle a woman's neck
with the intimacy and impermanence of a breath.

Already summer leaned its wide body over Basrah
and the day promised to be heavy and hot.
An argument flared outside the goldsmith shop next door.

I am Muslim and you are a dirty Mandaean.
You have no right to argue with me.

Like rough hands, the words grabbed Abu Ammar from behind
and shook him.
Their tone pulled him out of his chair.
Abu Ammar dropped the necklace.
Before he opened the door to his shop, screams reached him.

Outside, I found my neighbor on the sidewalk in a pool of blood,
a young man above him with a knife.
The murderer saw me, turned, and ran.
Other merchants came out.
There was no time to think.
We threw ourselves at him, subdued him,
took his knife,
and tied him up.

But the wrestling had barely begun.
Next day, the fresh-scrubbed, clear-eyed face of terror
visited Abu Ammar's goldsmith shop.

The leader of the young man's tribe came to me
because I was the first witness.
He asked me to change my statement.

"The young man," he said, "acted rashly.
Let us deal with this in our own way."
"How can I do this?" I said.

"The man he killed is a relative of mine.
And he was caught with the knife in his hand."

"You are a fool," he said.
"If you don't bend,
we will break you."

For Mandaean people,
vulnerability had long been a fact,
the threat of violence part of Earth's atmosphere,
a carcinogenic particulate in the air they breathed.

At trial, in October,
the air thick with smoke and ash,
another chance to bend:
without eyewitness testimony, no case.

There was plenty of time now to think,
but one thought prevailed:
It is not right that Mandaeans suffer such persecution, Abu Ammar said,
a rich vein of anger rising on his forehead,
flakes of gold in his narrowed eyes.
It is not right that we have our throats slit,
that we are slaughtered.
For this reason, I testified.

The tribal leader approached Abu Ammar as he left court
and offered him money to change his testimony.

Again I refused.
"OK," he said. "You have had your last chance.
There will be no more offers, no more negotiations.
We made every offer we could to preserve your life,
and you refused to accept."

Abu Ammar wiped his brow.

This worried me a great deal.
I spoke with my wife.
We were especially concerned, he said,
pausing and looking me in the eye,
for the safety and welfare of our daughters.

Violence is a storm fracturing homes,
scattering people like sticks.
Splitting up and moving in with relatives in three separate regions of
Iraq,
the family closed their shop and fled.

On the strength of Abu Ammar's testimony,
the court sentenced the defendant to death.

After this, other goldsmiths called and told me,
"Never come back. They will kill you."
I was afraid.
I believed there was no place in Iraq where I could be safe.
The Muslim tribes are vengeful.
Wherever I hid, the tribes, working together, could find me.

Abu Ammar's twin brother was murdered.

They came from behind,
Abu Ammar said, shaking his head,
and clubbed him.
I believe they mistook him for me.
I want to be clear that I do not know this for a fact.
It is my suspicion that they killed him thinking he was me.

In June of 2000, Abu Ammar fled, alone, to Jordan.

At the time, our children were still in school

and we wanted them to finish,
so my wife stayed behind with them in Iraq.
It is not a simple thing to flee your country.
It is not vacation,
a chance to rest, recoup, to travel,
to educate oneself.

From the moment I left, I worried about them.
For five years here in Jordan,
I thought about them and worried about how they were doing
and if they were safe.

And for those left behind . . .
It was terrible, Um Ammar said.
We lived in terrible fear,
especially after the invasion.

The volcanic overthrow of the Iraqi government
spewed millions of tons of ash and cinder into the environment.
In the lawless, polluted atmosphere following the US invasion,
the air became more and more toxic for Mandaeans,
the accumulating threats, kidnappings, murders
an organized purge.
We use the term "serial killer"
for patterned, related, multiple murders
by a single person,
and the two words are cold water rising above our waist, our chest,
cold hands on our throat.
But there is only one word
for the systematic killing of a people:
genocide.

For Um Ammar and her three children in Iraq,

the environment became uninhabitable in October of 2005,
when Zenen, the youngest daughter,
received a death threat.

At 2:00 pm,
while I was walking home from college on a busy street,
four men with weapons stopped me.
"Whore," they called me, and "Dirt."
They spat at me.
"We'll kill you if you don't wear a hijab," they said.
"We'll kill you if you wear tight pants."

They did this in the middle of the day, Um Ammar emphasized,
and on the main street!

Two days later,
one of Zenen's college friends was murdered.
A note left with her body served as a terrifying warning
to other women.

From that time until we arrived in Jordan, Zenen said,
leaning forward in her chair,
it was a nightmare,
her eyes daring me to imagine the dream she'd lived in,
her fist clenched, her chest heaving,
her words clipped,
each one a gold link in a chain,
the final word a clasp
and anger its semi-precious gemstone,
a necklace declaring,
We are here, whole, intact.
Against all odds, we've come through
together.

Balasem

Amman, Jordan
April, 2009

I

We heard him before we saw him,
his voice a hand dragging rocks off a pile
coming to us not from a deep well of the past
but from a walled-in cave, a hidden pocket in the present.

Don't talk about Baghdad!
Don't say the name of that place!

II

We found Balasem buried alive
in a typical al-Hashmi basement apartment
more hole than home,
yelling from a curtained back room,

They took our houses, our land . . . our sons!
I blame the Americans!

Above us, forbidden entrance,
a vigilant sun walked the earth.

III

You thought war was a bullet? A bomb?
No, a shovel, digging graves, burying people alive.
One handful of dirt and stone at a time
in your eyes, ears, mouth.

The militias drove us out, his wife says.
And when our son was killed, the shock was too much,
and Balasem had a stroke.

Adding another stone to the pile,
packing it with their small shovel,
even Red Crescent doctors write Balasem off as hopeless.

Balasem, we learn, was a famous horse trainer.
He was the first one the TV would call for an interview,
his daughter Dalal says.
Even after we fled to Jordan,
people looking to buy a horse called for his advice.

And now they bring us the incongruous photos,
contraband from a forbidden past,
images pointing to a time that has been disappeared,
that has no intercourse with the present:

Balasem, in mowed grass, his arm around a colt.
Balasem with Saudi princes and wealthy sheiks at a racetrack in Dubai.
Balasem with European horse owners in the winner's circle.
Again Balasem with the winning horse.
And again, flowers for Balasem.

The horses loved him, his wife says.
When he walked into the stables,
they would whinny and sing.

IV
Najlaa, who has been underground before,
followed the long fingers of his voice,
and pulling at the rock and rubble,
found him,
Balasem,
the horse trainer for princes and aristocrats,
in diapers
on his back on a mat on a cold floor.

He was embarrassed by the odor, Najlaa explained,
so I cleaned his bed,
and we sprayed perfume.

Maybe it's not so much courage that sees in the dark,
but compassion,
an intuitive knowing that the darkness is peopled
and hears its cries,
a physical intelligence, something alive in Najlaa's body itself
that leads her down into dust and rubble,
one hand reaching for another hand,
an eye seeking a face.

I massaged his back, Najlaa said.
He felt as though someone cared,
and he started praying for me.
This old man that I should help,
he began to pray for me.
He took my hand
and told me his story.

> *I started working with horses when I was six.*
> *I loved being with them.*
> *I loved the air and the sun and the grass.*
> *You can trust a horse.*
> *A horse will not deceive you.*
>
> *People will forget you, but not a horse.*
> *A horse will remember your smell,*
> *and if you treated him well,*
> *he will know you are a friend.*
>
> *I had the best stable in the country.*
> *The militias came.*
> *They occupied my homes.*
> *They took our land.*

Now we have nothing.
Even the horses ... even the horses are leaving Iraq.
They are being shipped to Egypt for money ...

I no longer have any sons.
I say to God, "You took them.
Give them back."

He cried, Najlaa told me.
He really poured his heart,
all of it.
By the end, we were both wet.

We lifted Balasem off the floor, out of the hole,
dressed him,
wheeled him outside.
Like an old friend, the sun embraced him.

Balasem Knows

Amman, Jordan
April, 2009

As though he has practiced all his life for this moment,
Balasem knows exactly how to be with me.

The old man who fell in love with horses
when he first began visiting their stables at age six,
who translated the language of his love into a life,
who trained racehorses for Saudi princes and European nobles
knows how to be with an animal he is meeting for the first time,
one who doesn't speak a word of Arabic.

Without preamble, almost as a greeting,
he says,

Never hit a horse.
Treat it kindly, and it will remember you as a friend.

And after a long pause,
his head nodding,
his eyes fixed on my eyes, caressing me,

People forget you,
but a horse remembers.

The man who watched as violence chewed and swallowed his two
grown sons,
who, fleeing death threats in Iraq,
rode his fate bareback at a gallop across the border into Jordan,
the man who stood tall among horses in Iraq and Dubai
is content to sit with me.

Here on the surface of the earth,
on a concrete patio above the squalid, underground cave of his apartment,

in the warm lap of an April sun,
we sit.
Balasem has slowed his bareback, breakneck mount
and dropped to the ground.
He steps into the cool stables of his past.

Come closer, he says to me.
And to his wife, *Turn my chair
so I can see him better.*

From his wheelchair,
his smiles pat me, rub me down,
blanket me warmly.
There is little to say.
It's his voice that matters.

A horse can smell you, he murmurs.
That is how he knows you.
The light of a thousand sunny days shines from his eyes.
Let the horse smell you, and he will know.

Odor of dirt and hay,
fragrance of fresh mowed grass
greet us.

My heart, leaning over its gated stall,
stamps its feet,
shakes its ragged mane,
whinnies, and sings.

I Never Stopped

Amman, Jordan
April, 2009

Najlaa speaks

I never stopped loving my fellow Iraqis,
even when bandits kidnapped me in Baghdad.

Here in Amman, I never stopped working for Iraqis,
even when someone accused me
of trying to convert people to Christianity,
even when Jordanian secret police followed me to my door,
even in their offices as they interrogated me.

I never stopped hearing a future where soft music played,
even when the present was filled with explosions and sirens
and people wailing.

We Questioned the President

Amman, Jordan
April, 2009

*Bush lied to us. He didn't tell us we were going to kill you. He didn't tell us
we were going to kill civilians . . . fathers, mothers, children . . .*
        —An American marine speaking confidentially to Abu Hassan in prison

Leaving our names behind
and arriving
armed, helmeted, suspicious
in the Middle East,
we were surprised to find the trees growing upright,
a familiar, temptress sun coaxing them,
their leaves green, their fruit sweet;
children like skeins of yarn tangling, untangling,
running in fields, in streets,
throwing rocks, kicking soccer balls,
the youngest straining to keep up with their elder siblings.
We were surprised to find mothers giving birth, fathers carrying their
infants;
on the streets, men greeting each other with kisses,
girls walking arm in arm, whispering, laughing,
boys growing out of their bodies,
the future laying out a welcoming carpet.
We were surprised to find
buses packed with passengers, baggage;
taxis honking;
gardens, houses, bedrooms, kitchens, tables, curtained windows.

Expecting to find only ourselves—
brigades, soldiers, suspicion—
we met people everywhere.
Bewildered, we questioned our guns,
but they could not explain themselves.
We questioned our faces,
but our mirrors were silent.

We questioned the landscape,
but it would not tell us what planet we had reached,
what dreamland we moved through,
whether nightmare or friend.

We asked our president,
but he could not tell us our names.

Internal Bleeding

outside Baghdad, Iraq
August, 2009

for Takashi and Kathy

Waleed, in place of your smile, your whitewater eyes,
your humming intelligence,
I have only questions.
Where are you?

The unbridgeable distance between us
is the clawed hand of a fetus tearing at my stomach,
a scream imprisoned in my mind, unable to be born.

Since you disappeared,
since a hole opened in the air and a tongue shot out, snatching you,
and now that I've learned that tongue is American,
that mouth a prison in Iraq,
questions, like enraged hornets, swarm and bite.
After eighteen months, is your mind intact,
your body,
your soul?
Are they torturing you?
How are Suad and your children managing?
And most important,
How do we reach you, help you climb out,
walk away?

The same gluttonous war that took your livelihood,
your home (how many times?),
your brother, mother, your cousin,
that took Suad's father, rolled him around in its mouth,
and spat him out for a ten-thousand-dollar ransom,
then took him again the following year—

the same war that swallowed you eighteen months ago

and in whose belly you rot and roll—

that same war keeps me from Baghdad,
cuffs my hands,
threatens me with dogs,
prods me with hot electric pokers,
beats my small white body red and blue.

I think of Waleed constantly.
                                    —Kathy Kelly

Now We Know

outside Baghdad, Iraq
August, 2009

I
Now we know, Kathy said,
and the wrecking ball swung free,
accelerated,
shattered my rib cage.
Now we know,
and the bullet spun out of its chamber.

Now we know Waleed's been in prison the last seventeen months.
Takashi helping Suad and the children make do without him,
Zaineb not yet a year old when the merciless US Marines
plunged into the village south of Baghdad,
crossed the river, waded through his okra fields,
and dragged Waleed and two brothers from their homes.

II
Waleed,
in the first days and weeks after your disappearance,
after you dropped into God-knows-what hole in Baghdad,
alarms sounded, flares ignited and flashed across the night sky,
and I could feel your hand in mine,
a warm light, warm blood glowing where our fingers met.

But the unspent fuel of wasted days accumulated,
the idle months between us combusted,
and the sky filled with smoke and ash and cinder,
the poisonous, impenetrable, scorched air of inaction.

For seventeen months,
neither giving you up for dead

nor believing you were still alive,
but accommodating myself to the growing darkness,
moving through it,
O! living in it.

I withdrew my hand.
Waleed, I forgot you.

If love is compassionate action,
then I stopped loving you.

III
But now,
now we know,
and the wind of three words has cleared the air.
Your face, Waleed, is a star guiding me.

Now, the pulse at my wrist, my neck, at my temple,
my very breathing speaks your name,
and the simple practice of listening
is a blue flame fueling action.

Alternative Art, Alternative Media

outside Baghdad, Iraq
August, 2009

Forget the US military *securing neighborhoods,*
troops entering *insurgent strongholds*
capturing *enemy combatants.*
Forget *war as liberation.*
Here's how it looked to Suad and her sister
and their young children
when Waleed and his two brothers were dragged off
through the fields to an American prison in Iraq.

The Marines came, *semper fidelis,*
faithful to boot camp,
to boots kicking in doors, kicking over lamps and chairs,
kicking furniture and toys and clothing,
tracking mud on floors and rugs and bedding,
faithful to boots pressed to the backs of Iraqi necks,
faithful to each other, yes,
but also to Rumsfeld and Cheney and Chevron.

And faithful to their battle plan,
they slithered through the okra fields,
bellies in the dirt,
and surrounded the houses.

Children woke to find snakes in their home,
snakes in their beds,
snakes coiled in corners, hissing unintelligibly,
striking at the bedposts and table legs,
striking at their fathers who lay face down on the floor
reptiles wrapped around their eyes, their wrists, their necks.

And then slowly, in full view of everyone,
their prey incapacitated,

the snakes unhinged their jaws,
opened their gaping mouths
and swallowed the adult males,
peristaltic waves moving men down those long throats.

Children froze in terror or hid their faces and wailed.
Women watched while the snakes, their stomachs engorged,
slithered away
to the safety of their lairs
to digest their take,
to sleep and dream.

Thank You

Jordan
September, 2009

Ghada,
today birds brought me song-filled ravines below your house.
September sun on stone spelled your name,
and wind, choreographing sunlight through olive branches,
brought terraced gardens above your home in Fuheis.

For three weeks within me I carried a cemetery,
a moonscape,
a dark side of a planet.
Of use to no one, sliding over the edge of an abyss,
I descended into a fanged and frosty darkness,
a tooth piercing my throat,
my voice withered, a hoarse whisper my only song.

But when you came to me today, Ghada—
not a mere memory of you greeting me
        outside the Plaza Mall in Amman,
your face outshining a mid-April sun —
but your actual presence,
a star around which I orbited,
your celestial light filled my house, my eyes,
my mind.

And when you came, Najlaa and Suad,
you who have crossed deserts and outrun cemeteries,
your laughter invaded me,
and the sure rope of your intelligence
lay beside me, a lifeline.

And when Mustafa came,
the missile's nine arms no longer wrapped around his legs,
at the sight of his winged spirit hovering beside me,

at the sound of his human voice,
I left my wheelchair.
I, too, stood,
my lungs filled with his clarion song.

And finally,
when I saw you, Yasir and Zena,
eleven-month-old Ammar in your arms,
I left the pit.
I climbed out into the warm and radiant embrace of your simple
home.

Afghanistan

Afghan Youth Peace Volunteer Mohammad Jan, left, and his brother Tooryalai and his three children

—photo by David Smith-Ferri

They Can Speak for Themselves

A nationwide *New York Times* / CBS poll, conducted in the run-up to US mid-term elections, revealed that only three percent of American voters identified the war in Afghanistan as a concern. At the time, the war had ground on for nearly nine years, the US government had spent a staggering three hundred billion dollars waging it, thirteen hundred American service members had died in it, and thousands of others had been physically and / or emotionally traumatized. The results of the poll were a testimony to both the severity of the economic hardship facing Americans and the success of the US government's efforts to control information coming out of Afghanistan and the discourse surrounding the war.

In a world where the weaponry of war is terrifyingly powerful and sophisticated and where its victims are overwhelmingly civilian men, women, and children, the need to restrain military forces and their governments and hold them accountable for their actions is urgent and imperative. The stakes are especially high in Afghanistan where the US military, the wealthiest and most powerful on the planet, is operating in a country that has lived with war for thirty years and where most people's lives are compromised by extreme poverty, malnutrition, and lack of access to quality health care, education, and reliable electricity.

Afghan people do not need Americans to speak for them. They can speak for themselves. But in a country torn by war, where a corrupt central government is accountable not to its people but to foreign powers, and where the majority of international journalists are embedded with foreign military forces, how do they find an audience, how do they amplify their voices?

I traveled to Afghanistan in October of 2010 as part of a small delegation organized by Voices for Creative Nonviolence because I wanted to speak directly to people in Afghanistan and to try to represent their voices in poetry. I had the opportunity to meet and talk with a range of men, women, and youth, including farmers in remote villages, refugee camp residents, hospital patients, businesswomen and businessmen, lawyers, university faculty and students, members of parliament, and international staff of nongovernmental organizations. In the poems that follow, I have tried to represent their voices.

Our delegation traveled at the invitation of a group of Afghan youth who have first-hand knowledge and experience of the ravages of war. Out of their pain and loss, they are crafting a vision of nonviolent social change in Afghanistan and have committed themselves to identifying and supporting non-military solutions to the conflicts in their country. Like their counterparts in Egypt, Tunisia, Libya, and elsewhere in the Arab world, they are trying to build support in their country for social reform. They are also building friendships and seeking support among internationals.

In a country where the government's intelligence forces are watching, where contact with foreigners can be a cause for suspicion and increased surveillance, and where travel from one province to another is dangerous, they take risks everyday.

As I write this, people in Egypt and Libya are risking their lives to create a better world for themselves and their children. Their courage and the courage of these Afghan youth create possibilities where none seemed to exist. Their courage also calls us to action.

The Right Messenger

from Ukiah, California
June, 2010

Last year, unexpectedly and without preamble,
Kathy invited me to travel to Afghanistan
to document, from the blunt end of the club,
the criminal impacts of war and violence
and to experience the hospitality
and humanity of Afghan people.

A white haze, a cold curtain of questions
familiar and unfamiliar
blinded me.

But when you died, Artis,
as I sought a way to know, a place to stand, a clear view,
the barometer fell
and a fierce wind rose
to scour my mind
and lift its thick blanket of confusion.
A sun shone unimpeded.
For the first time in months,
dawn gave the world definition, dimension.

When cancer in your brain
untied the moorings
and the small white paper raft of your body
floated from shore,
rocking, circling,
gaining a swifter current in the middle of the stream,
as it approached the edge
before pitching over and disappearing
into white swirling mist and foam,
a song escaped, reached me here.
It roused me, stood me on my feet.

When your eyes' blue crystal blaze dimmed,
when day and night became the same cold stone,
and the welcoming arc of your smile crumpled,
a hand found me and interlaced its fingers in mine.

That wind, that song, your hand . . .
The very thing I'd feared, mortality, comforted me,
led the way.

It was only later, the following week,
when the initial white wave of grief had fallen
and foamed at our feet
and returned to sea, leaving us drenched and empty,

it was only then that I recalled your placement
as a Peace Corps volunteer
had been to Afghanistan.

We Know Little

from Kailua-Kona, Hawaii
July, 2010

for Voices for Creative Nonviolence

Driving along the Kona coast of Hawaii,
we cross the unbreakable lineage of lava flows
from recent or ancient eruptions
that poured down volcano slopes—
long, lean bodies of molten iron and magnesium laying themselves
down,
burning the land,
building the island by destroying it.
The darker the flow the more recent,
the ores intact, the browns and reds of oxidized older flows absent.
It could take five hundred years for shy, infrequent, leeward rains

to crack the lava's code
and unlock its nutrients,
to open its doors and passageways to roots and claws,
soften it to soil,
and prepare a garden.

On the other side of the island, where Kilauea erupts,
lava transforms the moment it cools.
Daily rains work on magnesium and iron belched from miles below,
oxidize them,
and over a mere thirty years, a single generation,
turn them into soil where plants can root, grow.

But what of the black iron of war
even now being spewed on Afghanistan:
how many decades before it oxidizes and crumbles?
How many generations before iron bones clawing the land
loosen their hold, turn to soil?

We know little of concentrated ore in our own hearts
that prevents such questions from rooting there

and even less of the iron fingers of anger and fear
gripping Afghan hearts.

Less still about healing,
about horticultural arts appropriate to such soils,
to such a landscape, geography, climate, age.

Pondering Travel to Afghanistan

from Kailua-Kona, Hawaii
July, 2010

Again seeking a way to know,
I think, *Why shouldn't poetry lead us?*

Not the content of a specific poem, its lines
like cupped hands opening to reveal a truth about our lives,

its words marching before us
a road through mountains

or spreading above us, a tree in the tropics
showering white petals of wisdom,
aromatic, intoxicating.

No, but the hard fists of poetry balled within
yearning to unfurl in flowers,

the urge
somehow
against the bookie's odds

to be ourselves.

Yes

from Ukiah, California
September, 2010

for Jerica and Kathy, heading to Creech Air Force Base
and for Malik

If we don't say no

If we live in the shadow of lies
and fail to name them in public

If we see the missiles in our own backyards
and avert our eyes

If we hear,
oozing out of the rotten fruit of our government offices
that every Muslim man has explosives
strapped to his chest

If we hear the ticker tape of our daily news
mimicking the heartbeat of Pentagon policymakers

If we hear Afghan and Pakistani people described as
packs of dogs tearing at each other,
and we don't say no.

If we hear our neighbors say:

The whole world should just give up on these countries over there!
No one goes in or out for five years . . . PERIOD!
They'd all be dead in one year,
but let's let it sit for four years just to be sure! HA!

If we don't say no with our mouths,

with our paintbrushes and cameras,
our listservs and newspapers and magazines

If we don't say no with our bodies
by boarding planes and traveling to Afghanistan and Pakistan,
by standing in Islamabad, Kabul, Lahore,
by sharing tea,
by exchanging smiles, opinions, ideas

If we don't say no,
there will be no chance to say yes.

Preparing to leave for Afghanistan

from Ukiah, California
October, 2010

for Cynthia, Cathy, April, and the Iraq Peace Team

I
From the bottom of the ravine,
a pulsing chorus of frog song
like one voice
rushes into our yard
and enters my bedroom
through an open window
as though a heart were beating in the chest of the forest.

Lying in bed each night
as the fire of consciousness burns to embers,
small points of light—eyes—appear in the darkness around me.
Embers of wakefulness wink and waver,
but the eyes stare at me, unblinking
in growing darkness.

II
I am not one of the tiny troupe of nonviolent actors

who descended into the darkness of themselves,
down steep stairs cut in stone,
across moist caverns,
along private and winding passages only they can follow

who found there,
besides sulfurous gasses,
love bubbling at their core,
a self utterly intertwined with other selves
who lay down their bodies,

head to foot,
in an effort to narrow the distance
between them and people in Iraq.

I am not one of the clinically sane people

who came to Baghdad
in the winter and spring of 2003
as the beast of modern warfare
prepared to hurl itself on Iraq
and its terrified citizens

who played with young children
in the middle of the night
while Falcon-16 warplanes screamed overhead
and hellfire missiles exploded

who tried to distract those children,
cleaning and changing them when they wet themselves,
holding them in human arms
and listening as they ground their teeth in sleep

who, in the aftermath of each apocalyptic night,
volunteered in hospitals alongside Iraqi professionals
trying to stitch the world back together,
a world where Iraqi children arrived in pieces
and parents poured themselves
on impervious concrete floors.

Consent

flying from Dubai to Kabul
October, 2010

It begins with a glance from Kathy,
a raised eyebrow, a questioning smile.
A two-year-old across the aisle, Nasi—
small enough to fit in the plastic bag beside her—
looks back, wide-eyed, wondering,
waiting for a signal from within
and ventures a sign in the available common language,
a hand gesture,
a small Afghan finger tapping on the armrest of her seat.
Kathy, smiling, taps back.

What begins with a glance,
with a chance seating arrangement,
progresses rapidly into a game,
an exchange of signs and gestures.
And finally, as the plane climbs into a black night sky
leaving behind the false glamour of the airport
and its glitzy, duty-free shops,
it erupts into a rodeo.
Nasi, her hands alternately on her smooth, brown face
and behind her head
in her thick, black abundant mane of hair—
that hair that might be covered in public
for all of her adult life—
rocks forth and back,
strains the seatbelt around her waist,
shakes her head and neighs in delight,
fueled by a source she knows is bottomless,
the liquid black pool of her eyes locked on Kathy,
asking her consent.

Somewhere below, the Persian Gulf,

itself a dark eye,
watches us.
Ahead, the Hindu Kush shoulders the night.
Our plans, neighing in the private arenas of our hearts
and following the arc of the plane,
leap into darkness
and ask consent.

Beacon

UN Assistance Mission in Afghanistan helicopter, Kabul to Bamiyan
October, 2010

From any of the small, circular windows
like portholes
in the Soviet-era helicopter
churning through the mountains northwest of Kabul

From any of 999 points of view,
the mountains here are a desert,
sunstruck rock stretching to infinity,
windswept, sun-baked, a stone sea
without end,
storm-stirred, deep-troughed.
Behind every massive swell,
another, higher, dwarfing it:
parched, jagged ridges knifing into the sky,
reaching to the top of the world.
From the tops of five hundred stone waves,
nearly five hundred more.

But from the base of the thousandth wave, the impossible:
a swift river bending like an elbow
at the bottom of a steep ravine.
Along its arm and wrists, poplars,
and spilling from its hands
the promise of roads, homes, schools,
mosques, clinics, stores, farms, orchards, children.

In this immensity,
as the helicopter tops a final ridge and banks right
before the town swings into view,
there is nothing but the ocean of mountains exerting its claims,
the voluble river countering them,
the sun mediating.

And on the one, thin road
a single figure, indistinct and distant,
no more than a stick floating on a sea,
but moving, growing, living.
There! A man
on a bicycle,
sunlight flashing off his bike like a beacon
beckoning us to Bamiyan.

Imagine

Bamiyan, Afghanistan
October, 2010

The mountains deceived us,
telling stories only of tortured stone and uninhabitable heights,
and the conspiratorial UNAMA helicopter agreed,
a deafening roar of motor and blades
and sickening fumes of petroleum exhaust
disavowing all comfort.

Stiff and unsteady,
blinking in bright October sunshine,
we stepped down metal stairs onto Bamiyan's stony airfield.

Still unaware that the mountains
had quietly unzipped and emptied their pouches
to spread at our feet sequined rivers and creeks,
the orchards, wheat fields, gray-green willows, golden poplars, and
children
of Bamiyan valley.

As yet unable to see twelve boys lined up a hundred meters away
waiting to welcome us,
unaware they had already adopted us,
unaware such a capacity existed among strangers,
among youth, among people who have grown up with war.

Not yet able to imagine seventeen-year-old Faiz
waving from atop the steep, narrow, rocky trail to his home,
proud to show us his sheep and goats
then later, sobbing, head in hands
as he recalled the deaths of his parents when he was a child.

Fifteen-year-old Ali, whose brother, fighting in the north,
took his mother's mind with him.

Ali, holding my hand as men will do in Afghanistan
and walking me home in the dark.

Mohammad Jan expressing grief at suffering in other Afghan provinces.

Ten-year-old Ghulemai, whose mind and body still bear the handprint
of his uncle's disappearance after a bombing,
and Zekerullah recalling a horrible time
of people hiding in drainage ditches and potato storage bins.

Standing there in front of the helicopter,
I couldn't even imagine three minutes into the future
when fourteen-year-old Abdulai,
whose potato-farming father was killed by the Taliban,
would sling my heavy suitcase over his narrow back,
cheerful, confident of the common ground between host and guest,
defining himself by it,
drawing an unwavering line in response to my objections.
Smiling and joyful, he would tell me,
Don't worry. I am a mountain boy.

First Night

Bamiyan, Afghanistan
October, 2010

In Bamiyan, darkness does not deter us:
we walk unhurried through a sleeping bazaar.

But darkness,
on silent feet and lashing its tail,
stalks our hosts.

At dinner, words leaping out of him on clawed feet,
fifteen-year-old Ali asks,

Do Americans think we are animals?

Homeward, before a ten o'clock curfew,

I ask,

What makes you believe
Americans think you are animals?

Why else, Ali responds, *would they bomb us?*

Bamiyan Valley

Bamiyan, Afghanistan
October, 2010

for Kevin

Every day from a different angle,
the morning sun brushes the jagged ridgetop northwest of town,
gently drawing out pinks and reds and browns,
investigating crevices and ravines,
standing with millennial patience pondering outside caves.

Every day, every season,
the mountains and light converse,
a dialogue older than time,
the mountain revealing one thing
and holding others in shadow,
and the sun
slowly, gently
asking for more.

Syllables and broken phrases reach us even here,
even during work
as we farm on the valley floor.
A language we have known and not known
since the beginning of our people.

North Central Afghanistan

Bamiyan, Afghanistan
October, 2010

for Evan

Because they were here before there were people,
before trees, before insects, before life

Because their roots go down
into the fiery depths of the planet

Because they have held private counsel with the stars,
winter and spring,
for ages

Because they have absorbed the sun,
weathered snow,
outlasted storms,

the mountains believe that everything—
life, death, laughter, music,
planting and harvest,
rivers and lakes—
is theirs to bestow,
theirs to withhold.

Harvest

Bamiyan University, Afghanistan
October, 2010

Everywhere the road we take follows a river
or one of its nieces or nephews,
the one, unified, tribal family of water mothering all life.

In orchards,
apple trees emptied of their fruit turn yellow and gold.
In fields, farmers stoop and dig.
Golden potatoes,
distilled water and light,
stand upright in three-hundred pound plastic sacks.
After harvest, ox teams,
yoked as heavily as the farmers,
pull plowshares.

Following creeks upland
toward their sources in alpine snowfields,
we see families scything grass
or unearthing small, dry shrubs with heavy, wide-bladed hoes
then loading donkeys and transporting the harvest down to their
homes
and piling it against walls for use as fuel.

And everywhere and always the sun is thinking,
inviting relationship,
trying to know and understand the earth.

We step out of the sunshine and activity
and enter Bamiyan University.
In a seminar room at the Lincoln Center,
named for the sixteenth President of the United States
and funded by USAID,

we arrange ourselves around a circle of tables, filling every seat:
three Americans, twelve Afghan faculty and students,
the director of a local radio station,
and nine youth from local villages.

Kathy states our sense that US military actions in Afghanistan
fuel rather than dampen violence.

Switching metaphors,
the radio station host states that a US military presence,
like a protective reef,
keeps the Taliban at bay.

We suggest that
given the poverty we've seen,
money spent on electrical infrastructure, hospitals, jobs
would be a better bulwark against violence
than billions spent on the infrastructure of war.

A university administrator, smiling politely,
assures us the Taliban would
rise up like a storm surge and swamp the country.

Returning to our original metaphor,
we press back,
pointing out that even now,
like a fire underground
burning in the roots of trees and bushes,
violence spreads.

They laugh knowingly.
If the US left,
we would not even be able to meet here!

And so it goes, until, leaving the university,
seventeen-year-old Faiz pulls one of us aside.

I did not speak out
because I have been trained all my life
not to contradict my elders.
But I did have a question.
I wanted to ask,
I want to say:
"Aren't the Americans—
sweeping through villages,
staging night raids, firing missiles—
aren't they acting just like the Taliban?"

The Burqa Speaks

Bamiyan, Afghanistan
October, 2010

I

At home,
behind the mud-brick walls of your house,
beneath its wood and plaster roof,
upon its earthen floor,
you will be source and sustenance,
womb and breast,
flesh giving birth giving health to flesh.
You will be warmth,
radiant heat,
a star birthing other stars.
Like vines,
child and adult hands
will climb you for light, for life.
And every new face will be drawn from yours.

II

But in public you will disappear,
and the child who once wore your face,
the child who walked to school
with the sun on her brow, wind on her cheeks,
is dead.
A cold white sheet, you will be faceless,
less than a memory,
without past
without future
without substance,
a white shadow moving in front of fruit stalls,
over pomegranates, apples, almonds.

I will do this to you.
It is my job.

Sutures

Bamiyan, Afghanistan
October, 2010

If roads are sutures
binding wounds,
holding back past bloodletting,
then the knots are unraveling.

In 2002, Farid says,
at the beginning of the Karzai reign,
we could travel anywhere.
Now, you cannot travel
and the security is worse everyday.

If roads are cords
thrown over mountains, bridging rivers,
tying together provinces, cities, peoples,
binding a divided land,
then the ropes are frayed
and in some cases snapped.

Even when I travel a short distance
from my office here in Bamiyan
to the central office in Kabul,
I must be careful.
I leave behind all evidence
of my government job,
papers, identifications, files.
I leave behind my education.
I dress simply. Otherwise,
well, if they recognize me,
they will take me.

If the roads are arteries,
delivering oxygen, nutrients, antibodies,

then there are clots in the country's limbs,
a stroke waiting to happen.

I grew up in Gazni,
where many Hazara people live.
But now, the road from Kabul to Gazni
takes you through a Pashtun area.
They control it.
I have not been home
in five years.

Wonder

Bamiyan, Afghanistan
October, 2010

East of town, our van leaves the main road
and turns south onto a pitted dirt track
that crosses a river and follows a narrow creek
running through steep, red-rock ravines
sculpted by wind and water.
A land at once forbidding and inviting.

In every direction,
we find rock walls facing us, waiting,
offering us their example of endurance,
inviting us into their experience of eternity.

At a cutout in the road,
our van stops
and Mohammad Jan asks,
Would you like to walk to my house from here along the river?
Alongside the road
sits a rock with a symbol in white paint
attesting that the area has been cleaned of landmines.
We disembark
and set out on foot for Mohammad Jan's home.
Skirting adolescent apple orchards
and in the crooked arm of the creek,
a swath of lush, green plots planted in peas,
ripe and ready to be picked, we cross
plowed fields of newly harvested potatoes.

For forty minutes, we follow the creek
lined on one side with gray-green willow and golden cottonwood
trees
fluttering and flickering lazily.
On the other side, iron-rich rocks rise in a cliff

straight from the water's edge.
Cows and donkeys chew languidly on grass.
Sunlight, pouring into the valley,
raises the temperature into the mid-seventies,
and autumn's sweet dream of maturation and abundance
soaks us.

We leave the valley floor,
and climb onto the benchland
where Mohammad Jan's house sits
with a view above the cliffs
and into an infinity of mountains.

His older brother Tooryalai,
a tall Tajik man with thick, shoulder-length black hair
and wearing a white robe that hangs to his feet,
welcomes us with a broad smile
and leads us into his family's home.

We sit on pillows against the walls.
Tooryalai unrolls a long, red mat on the floor in front of us,
and Mohammad Jan and Faiz cover it with plates and food:
whole wheat bread in large, oval, unleavened loaves
that we tear with our hands,
platters of homemade wheat noodles,
fried potatoes, local apples, and bottles of orange soda.
If you weren't vegetarians, Faiz whispers to me,
we would have gone fishing this morning.

If there had been anxiety or ambivalence
about having westerners as their guests,
if they had argued
or wrestled with anger or bitterness as they prepared
for visitors from the country that invaded their homeland,
if there was any hesitancy, any holding back,
there is no evidence of it.

Mohammad Jan's mother joins us.
In 1998, she tells us, *violence came to this valley.*
We had to flee in winter, in deadly cold and snow,
in the dark.
It was terrifying.
I carried one of my children on my back the whole time.
In their desperate attempt to escape along steep mountain tracks,
some villagers perished from exposure,
others died after falling off a trail into a ravine.

Tooryalai cuts the tension in the room by joking,
War is the only time Afghans wonder why we have so many children.
You have to put one on a donkey, one on your back,
one on your shoulders . . .

The family fled a hundred miles on foot to Kabul
and lived there for four years.

Did anyone help you? Kathy asks.

Her question is greeted with wry laughter.
There were so many refugees that no one paid any attention to us,
Tooryalai says.

How did you survive? we ask.

We organized ourselves to sell things, explains Mohammad Jan,
who was eight years old at the time.
We worked as street vendors and in the market,
and we used the money to buy flour to make bread.

During their absence,
their home in this mountain village
was occupied by a political militia.
Even though we had to flee our homes for four years, Mohammad Jan
says,

and it was terrible not being able to give people a proper burial,
having to leave the bodies with just a few rocks on them,
we are thankful now for this time of relative peace.
But we know that there are people in other provinces that are in conflict,
and things there have not changed,
have not improved for them.

The day before,
we packed lunch, piled into two vans,
and drove to Band-e-Amir
where a necklace of six turquoise and sapphire lakes
studs the chest of mountains high above Bamiyan.
We stood astonished
at the ability of water to transform a landscape,
at its persistence in an otherwise barren terrain.

But now sitting in Mohammad Jan's home,
I am no less astonished by his family,
their riverine tenacity in the face of war and displacement,
the deep well of their hospitality and decency,
the oasis of their compassion for other Afghans.

Sipping tea
at the end of our meal,
we ask,
What should we say to Americans when we return home?

Tell them, Tooryalai says,
to come to Afghanistan and make friends.

Afterward

Bamiyan, Afghanistan
October, 2010

Afterward,
as he debates with Lala and Faiz
about the unaffordable price of a dowry

Afterward, while he sits on a rock
laughing with the others,
we will wonder
at the tight fist of memory
holding and releasing experiences and emotions

Afterward, we will wonder at the power of words,
of voice
to define and elevate a person.

But now,
as three Americans like mountains ring him,
waiting for him to speak,
Khamad Jan shrinks,
withdrawing into his small-boned, five-foot-one-inch body.

Sunlight flashes from aluminum vents
rising from an underground potato storage shelter,
its mortared, tight-fitting, granite masonry a single unit.
But standing on top of the shelter,
Khamad Jan seems to lose substance,
to break up,
light to pass through him.

The weight of the moment presses him.
His chest heaves.
He blinks and shakes his head.
More than once he seems ready to give up.

When I was young, he explains,
I was a good student.
I liked learning.
But now I can't seem to think.
War does this to your mind.

The oldest of six children,
Khamad Jan was only ten
when his father was kidnapped and killed by the Taliban,
when adult responsibilities landed on his shoulders,
when violence erupted, spewing ash and cinders
on the hillsides above his home,
and inside him a molten column of anger rose.

Sometimes I feel like I am going to explode.

But this isn't what he wants to tell us,
this passing, personal note.
He wants to say something lasting
with words that will burn themselves into the landscape of our minds,
something definitive about war.

We tell ourselves,
If you want to learn about the effects of war,
go to the people who disproportionately bear its costs.
And so we wait.

The sun inches across the sky
and his words rise.
War, Khamad Jan says, *destroys people.*
It destroys our livelihood.
It damages our minds.

He pauses, again waiting for words.
We, too, wait.

All the players in this war have their own purposes for being here.
There is absolutely no benefit to the people here
from the wars that are being fought.

I do not know if mountains in their aeries notice
or if stars behind a cloud of daylight see it,
but afterward,
Khamad Jan stands taller,
and sunlight, reflecting off his face and brow,
warms and illumines us.

You Are Not Alone

Bamiyan, Afghanistan
October, 2010

In Bamiyan city,
in plain view of mountains,
in a small room on the second floor of the Zuhak Hotel,
above the bazaar, above the noise,
above a steady flow of donkeys and bicycles and NGO trucks,
smoke and smell of roasting kabobs
climbing in through a hole in a window,
four Afghan youth huddle around a single cell phone.

They lean over each other,
and out of their bodies they build a tent, a place apart.
Within it they open a flap and welcome Anees
at the Rachel Corrie Center in Gaza
and through a Skype connection initiated in the US,
his voice enters the room.

Our house has been bombed four times, Anees says.
We have often slept wearing our shoes.

Fourteen-year-old Abdulai responds,

Anees, the situation here in Bamiyan is better than in Gaza.
Bamiyan is more secure than other Afghan provinces.
Kandahar would be similar to Gaza.

All occupations, Anees says, *are the same.*
In my family we worry, if we lose our house, where will we go?
Still we must ask, what about others?
People's homes have been destroyed.
They have no funds to rebuild,
so after moving into schools and mosques,

they are now looking for apartments.
We thank God we have been able to repair our house.

Fifteen-year-old Ali leans over and speaks into the phone,
and Hakim translates, his voice near full volume,
each carefully enunciated word
offered whole and distinct.
Anees, Ali says, *if bombings start again near your house,*
please go someplace else!

Come to Afghanistan! eleven-year-old Ghulemai says.

I have no permission to leave Gaza, Anees explains.

I understand, Abdulai responds.
My family ran from the Taliban.
My father was captured and killed by the Taliban.

Like a fire built from wet twigs,
the smoldering connection with Gaza smokes and sputters
and fails repeatedly.

One after another,
the Afghan boys lean over and speak into the small phone,
blowing on the coals,
repeating their messages again and again
until they get through.

Something shifts in Anees.
OK, he says, *I will tell you more of my story.*
During a bombing, my friends and I fled our homes,
but one friend decided to go back for something.
A missile exploded.
Everyone was frantic,
running to get people to a hospital.
Our friend disappeared.

Afterward, people asked me:"Didn't you see him?
Didn't you find him?"
Nobody knows what happened . . .
Many people here face this kind of uncertainty.

When our village was being attacked, Zekerullah recalls,
it was a terrible time.
People tried to hide in drainage ditches
and in potato storage shelters.
A horrendous time.

My uncle disappeared after a bombing, Ghulemai says.
He was never found.
Did he live?
Is he in prison?
To this day, we feel the pain.

During one attack, Anees says, I was separated from my family.
Afterward, I couldn't go back
because tanks were stationed outside the door of my home.
But I had to find out if my family was okay.
I was like a crazy person approaching the tank.
"I have to do something" I thought.
"If they want to shoot me, they can . . ."

My uncle, Zekerullah responds, was shot.
His body was full of holes.
It was a terrible situation, like what you have just described.

Anees, please remain strong and brave, Ali says.
We will endure this together, with you.
If it's beyond enduring, please call us.
Life will pass, but if it's beyond enduring, call us.

We will always be with you, Abdulai adds.
Please call. Never lose hope.

We share your pain, says Ghulemai.
Please don't give up.

And Zekerullah closes the conversation with
Please take care of yourself, Anees.

Mountains watch,
the sun proclaims its approval,
rivers murmur assent.

Why We Came Here

Kabul, Afghanistan
October, 2010

In dusty Kabul,
six fruitless trips in five days
across town to the Pakistan Embassy, seeking visas.

In and out of the metal gate at the ALT Guest House
exchanging smiles with armed guards in military camouflage,
young men who greet us
easily bearing assault rifles like laptop cases
slung from straps over their shoulders.

Dipping and rising like a ship through troughs in the pitted, unpaved streets,
we drive past endless construction
and street vendors with loads of pomegranates
poured on wooden carts like exotic red sea creatures dumped on deck
or small, unstable hills of toasted almonds.
Past the Herat Restaurant, Wahid's Pharmacy, Spinney's,
the Kabul Business Center.
Past the young boy hanging large, long, oval loaves
of unleavened bread like suits from nails in a local bakery
and the flayed carcasses of sheep hanging from hooks outside a shop,
a row of severed heads and a stack of fleeces beneath them on the sidewalk.

Churning through heavy traffic
and past teams of hard-shelled street children
attaching themselves like barnacles
to a car door with one hand
while the other hand wipes a window with a soiled rag
or taps on it with a fingernail
and a practiced look of pleading with lamb's eyes.

Along scrolls of battered, annotated streets with
guards holding assault rifles written repeatedly into their margins.

Through police checkpoints,
their long, thick metal bars blocking the road
and opening like jaws to admit us.

To arrive here
again
at the embassy
and sit under watchful eyes of Afghan military posted at the gate
and curious eyes of US military
sauntering back and forth to a grocery store
and plump, dusty myna birds strutting beneath rolls of razor wire high
atop barricades,
the most prominent architectural feature in the city.

All of this, only to be denied again and again,
to be blindfolded by a foreign language
and spun round and around by foreign rules remotely understood,
to be laughed at, to be objects of derision,
to learn in moments that flay like a scalpel,
what it is to lose our skin,
not to be ourselves.
Not to be privileged, American.

Dinner with Asif

Kabul, Afghanistan
October, 2010

Asif tells a story

Some things you don't forget.
A week into the US invasion,
and we understood the simple musical score of the war.
Every horrible night the whistling of precision bombs
and a timpani of ferocious explosions.
Each morning,
waking to a long, low-pitched, deep-throated exhalation of relief
from a city that had held its breath all night,
a city surprised to find itself alive,
still capable of breathing.

But then, in the late morning of the eighth day,
while I stood with a friend a block from my home,
an unexpected variation,
a daytime intrusion of the night theme with its kettledrums.
A sudden US warplane swooped out of a blue, October sky
over rooftops
so close,
so close, I tell you,
I could see the pilot.
He fired two missiles,
one a direct hit on a truck trying to escape,
instantly ending the music of its seven passengers.
The other missile,
with a purpose we could not discern,
uprooted a large tree across from our home
and in a terrible display of ferocity
threw it one or two hundred meters,
leaving a hole large enough to bury our car.
Right outside our house!
I was so scared, I kicked my sandals off

and ran home barefoot.

I was eighteen years old.
A week later, our family fled the country
to Peshawar, Pakistan.
Only my father remained.
I will not leave my home, he said.

There are some things you can't forget.

Noor

Kabul, Afghanistan
October, 2010

I

Surely Kabul has the worst roads
of any capital city on the planet.
Blacktop scarcer than electricity,
than chubby children,
dust stirred by traffic on unpaved roads
coating everything—
plants, buildings, lungs—
with a thin layer of fine, brown dirt.

On five short blocks
between the Afghan Logistics Guest House
and Noor's home,
though we see no other moving vehicle,
our car never drives above five miles per hour.
Instead, we plod along
making full use of the available roadway,
driving now on the right side,
now on the left,
depending on the size and location of ubiquitous holes,
at one point angling left
and squeezing past a six-foot-high rock pile
that occupies two-thirds of the street,
coming to full stops in front of craters
and tipping gingerly into them before rising again unscathed,
as though cars were mechanical turtles.

II

Inside his simple, mud-brick home,
Noor seats us on the floor
and on glass plates in front of us
he puts dried apricots like gemstones,

fresh-cracked walnuts,
a royal mound of pomegranate seeds
ruby-red and impossibly sweet.

The shattered roads and broken buildings recede.
And out of the mineral-rich depths of his past,
Noor spreads jeweled stories at our feet.

My family prized education.
We saw it as a bridge to a positive future,
not only for ourselves but for our country.
But we didn't anticipate the forces that would erupt
and shatter the foundations of our society.

I trained as an agronomist.
My oldest brother became a nuclear scientist,
working with Cobalt 60 in the early days of cancer treatment,
building a research lab at the university here in Kabul.
Another brother was an engineer.
They both trained in the Soviet Union,
maintained contacts there.
In the late 1970s, they picked up on the likelihood of an invasion,
and they talked about it.
When the Russians overthrew our government,
they stripped my oldest brother of his position and blacklisted him.
Without work, without a career,
he joined the resistance.
And they caught him.
All we know is that he was taken
to the outskirts of the city,
executed, and bulldozed into a mass grave.
We never learned anything more.
They also killed my two other older brothers.
But you have to multiply this many thousands of times.
After thirty years of war, tens of thousands of times.
In Afghanistan, every family has these stories.

III
Noor's two young sons bring trays
with bowls of creamed cauliflower soup
and hot tea.
Sprinkle pomegranate seeds in the soup, Noor says
looking up after leaning over a bowl to taste it,
steam rising into his face.
You will love it.

IV
We do not know what life will ask of us,
what bridges we will need to build with our bare hands
and cross,
what countries our soul will have to dwell in.

At the time of the Russian invasion,
I lived in Britain and worked as an organic farmer.
I was happy.
When word reached me that my brothers had been killed,
I knew something had to be done for their wives and young children.
It was a sleepless time,
a time of worrying how to make this happen.

Then, The Guardian *newspaper*
advertised an Austrian relief agency seeking an Afghan person
to live in Peshawar
and make three trips a year to Afghanistan.
I applied,
and the relief agency tried to talk me out of it!
Noor laughed.
"Don't worry," I said. "I know what I'm getting into."
"I know your family" the Afghan administrator of the program said.
"The Soviets will kill you."
"What about you?" I said. "They haven't killed you."
You see, he was taking the same risks I planned to take.
He didn't argue with me any further.

They gave me the job.
I rented an apartment in Peshawar,
and I began to visit my brothers' families.
Then I rented a house
and started bringing them, one at a time, to Peshawar, seeing to the
children's education and their medical care.
Now, all of these nieces and nephews have families of their own.
Sometimes we have reunions.

V
There was a time in Afghanistan when we had nothing.
Only bread and potatoes and seasonal foods,
sometimes kabobs.
No salt, no sugar.
And we learned to enjoy food without seasoning
and how sweet foods are on their own.

The future,
which once slept soundly in our bodies waiting to be woken,
troubled us with its fitful sleep.

We lived day to day,
not knowing when the Taliban would come,
only that they would take me if they found me.
What kind of a world have we created
where families are under such threat?

Whenever word came,
I fled to the mountains for a few days
and slept under a rock
until the threat passed.
When this boy, he said, pointing to eleven-year-old Sarroub,
was less than two years old,
word came to flee,
but the child was ill, feverish and dehydrated.
He needed a doctor, medicine.

"You must go, Noor," they said
and they forced me.
And my heart broke.
What kind of world is it
when an innocent child cannot get the medicine he needs to live?

In the mountains, feverish with worry,
I couldn't sleep,
sure the boy wouldn't live through the night.
Early in the morning,
a man came from our village.
"Please tell me the truth," I said.
And he was laughing. "How is Sarroub?" he laughed,
repeating my question, his eyes dancing.
"When you left the village,
the grandfather gave him a spoonful of olive oil.
Two hours later another spoonful,
and at three am, he woke his brother to play!"

Today, we think about people in Kandahar
where the US is acting just as the Taliban did,
going from home to home on night raids,
rounding people up like animals, dragging them away.
Why do they treat us like animals?

VI
In 2002, in the remote Panjshir Valley
high in the Afghan mountains north of Kabul,
we conceived a plan.
We incubated, hatched, and raised it.
It was a story of development,
feathered and winged,
and we dreamed it would fly
to every province in Afghanistan.
A story of local shuras acting as community development councils,
of governance at the grassroots,

of local ownership of issues and processes.
We were giddy with the possibilities.
It would be our Islamic democracy,
not to compete with Western democracy
but to stand alongside it.

Whether literate or not, people in Afghan villages
are very capable of analyzing their local situation,
of creating councils that work together and choosing leadership.
I have seen it.
And from there you can move on to larger governance structures,
all the way to the parliament.
You wouldn't believe the analyses and solutions
people come up with when they are addressing local issues.
Believe me,
they are beyond what a central government could even imagine.

And when the World Bank came to Panjshir,
when they saw what was being accomplished,
when they stepped in with funding, saying
"We will make this a model for all of Afghanistan,"
we threw our arms out and hugged each other.
We dreamed. Oh, yes, we dreamed.
We thought we'd see our story fly to the rest of the country,
but it never left the ground.
They clipped its wings,
broke one of its legs, stuffed the lame bird in a cage,
and paraded it around the country.
They paid people to reproduce it,
paid them to clip its wings,
to build the cage,
to break its leg.

A community development process,
one that builds a base with transparency and fairness,

could give life to the people of Afghanistan,
could restore dignity and local control,
could revive the soul of our nation.

Instead, they turned it over to the NGOs.
Today in Afghanistan, development aid is aimed at taking pictures
and producing a report.
The World Bank team is looking for figures:
"How many trees did you plant?"
They are not interested in process.
They put the tangible result,
not the people,
at the center.

And they come with ready-made plans.
We receive their orders:
"This is the project. Implement it."
No local involvement in assessing needs, developing solutions.
Before setting foot in Afghanistan,
they've got it all figured out!
How can that be?
Aren't they interested in what Afghan people think and know?
The US leadership needs to be educated,
but they don't want to learn.
I meet people from US Provincial Reconstruction Teams
and they think they know better than Afghan people.

He paused and looked at us.
They act exactly like Russians.

The aid agencies' perspective is that, because they are paying us,
we should shut up and play the game.
This is not right.
And what happens when people are gagged
and told to play along?
They are in it only to get what they can for themselves.

Everyone, from President Karzai on down, is holding out a hand
saying, "Give, give, give."

If we had taken one quarter of one quarter of one quarter
of the billions that they've spent,
we could have funded a real process of community development.
Instead, we've lost our dignity, our soul.

VII
Noor looked at us.
There's nothing in education in Afghanistan today.
You can put up a building and give it a name,
but that doesn't make it a school.
We can talk about teacher training,
but there is nothing to show for it.
We suffer to see our children asking for something more.

Fourteen-year-old Ahmad,
the oldest of Noor's four children,
sat down with us.
My children are smart, Noor said.
They're talented.
And I cannot give them what they need to develop.

Silence settled on us.
He looked at his hands
then at us.
And thirty years of war festered in the room,
in the walls, in the hearts and minds of occupants
sick and tired of being occupied.

Earthquake

Kabul, Afghanistan
October, 2010

Here in Kabul,
wind rises,
trees, previously sane, thrash and tear at themselves,
and dust like an invasion envelops the city,
turning its air a sickening brown,
blotting out a blue sky, the sun, the pale, white petal
of a late-afternoon moon floating above eastern hills.
We welcome each other's presence nearby.
We feel the ground solid and sober beneath us
and trust it.

In the US,
news from Afghanistan comes to us in bytes and pixels,
words and images,
a dust storm of military analyses and strategies,
but after nine years of occupation,
what is our proximity to Afghan people?
Can we sense them nearby?

Today, an Associated Press article blew in
with this assessment,
looking to clear the air
and provide a stable ground upon which to stand:

The Kandahar operation, launched last month . . .
has so far produced stunning results.

But yesterday,
Leila, direct from Kandahar,
entered our room like an earthquake.
Five years ago, with only a head scarf,

I traveled with three men in a car.
A long trip from Kandahar to Uruzgan,
and then, on a remote road,
the car stuck for hours, sunk like a dinosaur in the mud.
We never worried for a moment about our safety.

Today, in Kandahar city,
my home is a three-minute car ride to my office.
But for fear of making that trip,
I moved into the office with my daughter.

Her words shook the ground.
A friend of mine came home in a rickshaw,
stopped outside her home for two minutes to greet a neighbor,
and in that time, in those perilous moments,
a gunman on the back of a motorcycle
pulled up and shot her in the head.
The guys who killed her are still roaming around the city.

Her words turned the ground to water and submerged us.
There is so much pain in Kandahar.
The moments and hours
come to us like sheathed knives,
and we do not know until they pass
whether they will leap from their covers
and strike someone we love.

She entered our hearts.
Last week a car full of ammunition exploded,
and the whole city felt its impact.
My nine-year-old cousin heard us gasp
and wonder aloud what could have caused it.

"It sounded like a truck full of dynamite," he offered.
A nine-year-old should not learn to make these judgments.

She slipped into our bloodstream:
Negotiate with the Taliban?
If it means peace, yes.
I'll meet with Mullah Omar.
If it means peace, take me.

What We Hear

Kabul, Afghanistan
October, 2010

I
In Afghanistan,
the difference between hearing and seeing
can be measured in lives.
It is the difference between talk and action,
between a promise and delivery on it.

High in the Afghan mountains,
in a village of illiterate subsistence farmers,
seventeen-year-old Zerghuna has no trouble finding words
to describe it.

We hear a lot about aid and development for women,
but it is all tongue, all talk.

Her words are white water.

What aid? What development? Where is it?
Those agencies should come here and see.

II
Leila pulls the veil off what it can mean to be a woman
in the conservative Pashto culture
predominant in southern Afghanistan.

In Kandahar
even after the Taliban were overthrown in 2001
attitudes toward women as property persist.

Beginning at age seven or eight,
a girl is discouraged from going out

and she can't do so without a scarf.
At puberty, she must wear a burqa
and be accompanied in public by an aunt or older woman.

But that is only the public face,
the most well known aspect
of her servitude.

In Pashto culture,
you get the girls married as early as you can,
and they have children until they are unable to.
A woman can have eighteen children.
I've seen it.

Leila describes the making of a servant class.

A woman delivers babies, cooks, cleans . . .
and works in the service of men.
This is her main job.

Men hold her life in their hands.
From the day she is born
she is at the mercy of her father,
and at marriage she goes under control
of her husband and his family.
If she has a lot of sons,
she may enjoy some status,
but as they approach puberty,
these same sons also begin to control her.
Some man has to control the woman.
So she never really knows freedom.

III
There are exceptions.

My father has let me do anything in life that I wanted to do.

He is an educator.
He believes in giving opportunity.

We were five daughters,
and my grandmother pressured my father to get another wife,
one who would bring him a son.
My dad loved my mother.
He never gave in to the pressure.

IV
After the Soviet invasion,
our family fled across the border to Pakistan.
We built one of the first houses in a refugee village called New Quetta.
Over time, people poured in
and with them came the Jihadis,
the mujihadeen.
In southern Afghanistan, people will kill for God.
My sister and I were the only girls in the village who went to school.
We were in second and third grade.
Some men in the village believed girls shouldn't go to school.
At a meeting, they discussed throwing acid in our faces.
Luckily, a man who knew my father convinced the others to wait.
"Their father is a reasonable man," he said.
"If he's willing to take them out of school, we won't harm them."
My parents took us out of school.
A year and a half later, through UNHCR,
we came to the US as refugees.

V
In 2003 when I prepared to return to Kandahar,
people tried to talk me out of it.
My father said,
"Do what you want to do."

VI
When we ask Leila about protecting women's rights

as a justification for continuing US military operations,
a cloud bursts.
A torrent of words falls, gathers, runs.
Creeks form. A river swells.
Those words, those waters
run in us still.

VII
It's not a woman thing anymore, Leila says.
People are being killed left and right.
And what is the US doing?
Raiding people's homes at night
and running aerial bombing campaigns.
Think about it from the perspective of an illiterate woman in Kandahar.
Thirty years ago she saw the Russians flying warplanes overhead.
Now there are American warplanes
and she's supposed to see a difference?

Standing up, taking a breath she says,
OK, people aren't going to like this.
A few months ago, I went to a big conference in Europe,
and an Afghan woman received an award.
And in her acceptance speech
she talked about the great progress
that has been made over the last nine years.
She urged Americans not to negotiate with the Taliban,
or everything would be lost.
"On behalf of women in Afghanistan," she said,
"we're really grateful for the support of First World feminists."
And one by one people stood and cheered.

I was hurt by this, by all the applause.
What do they know?
Not that I'm a fan of Talibs,
but where I live
women suffer the loss of loved ones on a daily basis.

For us, the loss of a loved one means more
than the loss of rights.
When people say, "Take off your burqa,"
the women I know will say, "What are you talking about?
It's my children that matter."

I've seen too many mothers cry.
Seriously, there is so much pain in southern Afghanistan
but no one knows about this.

At the moment a bomb explodes or a missile strikes,
do I care about my rights? My burqa?
No, I care about my child growing up without war and violence.

Yes, some Kabuli women dance to the claps of feminists
from Europe and America.
But if it means my child will have a safer future,
I'm willing to step over some of my rights.

Predator Drones

Kabul, Afghanistan
October, 2010

for Barbara and Barry

1
The truck,
from the moment it entered the bird's line of sight,
cannot be understood as anything but an alien terror,
a thing not merely out of its experience
but beyond its genome,
beyond a red-tailed hawk's worst nightmare.

If we think otherwise,
we have not spent long enough as birds
contemplating that experience.
There was a time
when this form of "crossing over" was common,
when people labored to inhabit the mind of "the other,"
to understand
and to be transformed.
And from this a sense of kinship arose
that could not be easily shaken.

We do not know much of what the bird had been doing
in the half hour before it tried to cross the four-lane highway,
weighing a full-grown rabbit in its talons.

We know the truck, according to its nature,
had been hurtling at highway speed
for twenty-five miles,
tearing through air,
compressing it in front and stretching it behind,
following the millennial contours of the river

that dodged or leaped over boulders
and carved granite into shelves and walls.
And somehow, as though guided by an invisible hand,
it came out of a long bend in the road
just as the great bird,
laboring under the weight of its prey,
reached the same exact spot,
leaping moments earlier from a tree branch
to exit the riparian corridor
and falling in two successive, drooping arcs
almost to the level of the pavement,
its wings working furiously,
the shifting weight of the dead rabbit
throwing it off balance
and dragging it down.
That the truck had not set out to harm the bird
was nowhere in evidence.

II
To be known is one thing.
By day, the sun embracing us.
And at night, stars and planets and moons,
a thousand thousand eyes
from thousands of light years
silently observing . . .

The trees standing and watching,
blinking their thousand eyes in the sunlight,
swaying as though under water,
always there,
outside windows, at the edges of sight,
leaning above us,
their vast intelligence wrapping us.

The mountains, shoulder to shoulder,
mothers, fathers, aunts, uncles

uplifting skies,
nearly wordless,
knowing us from the beginning.

But now the desert, too, has eyes.
No, not the desert, but a thing in the desert.
A thing in North America, on an Air Force base,
behind fences and gates and locks,
in a building,
a bank of computers in a warren of offices.
In the desert where no one will see it,
it can see us.

But it doesn't know us.
It has never known us.
It doesn't even know our names.

III
In Afghanistan, clouds carry bombs,
and no one can predict the weather.

IV
Viewed from the understanding of people living in Afghanistan,
there may be no reason to describe a Predator Drone
as anything less or more than an unholy horror,
a thing with no purpose but to destroy,
a mechanical creature beyond the sure wisdom of our bodies,
beyond the memory even of our DNA,
a creature wholly unnatural
and utterly without rights on this earth.

Smoke

Kabul, Afghanistan
October, 2010

After meeting Leila
and breathing the acrid smoke of her words
about violence and fear in Kandahar,
I dreamed I stood in a blank, white, empty room
facing a door locked from the outside.

Smoke, at first in slender fingers
then full-bodied and thick,
entered from under the door
and rose, climbing into my face.

They are trying to suffocate us, I said
to an unidentified, unseen someone behind me.

From the torn corner of a large, rectangular bag
heaved over my back and bending me,
I began to pour white sand through gray smoke,
a fine trickle
onto the floor beside the door
until the entire length of the seam was sealed
by a small embankment of sand.

Kneeling, I dug my fingers into the sand,
testing it, assuring myself that smoke would not penetrate.

To the left of the door,
the wide-eyed walls met at a crisp right angle,
a clean, straight line, ceiling to floor.
They radiated their own bright, sterile, surgical light,

a light without end
in a room without dreams, without sleep.

Standing, facing the door, I thought,
What will they try next?
the words invading my mind like slender fingers,
curling in corners, choking the air
like smoke.

The Center

Charahi Qamber Refugee Camp
Kabul, Afghanistan
October, 2010

I
Kabul, crippled and unkempt,
drags its lame left leg up the hills,
a city swollen in nine years
from one-and-a-half to five million.
Sixty percent of the people are squatters,
constructing one-room, stick-and-mud homes
without electricity,
without plumbing,
wherever they can.

In Charahi Qamber
on the expanding, tumorous western edge of the city,
on the main road, past the National Assembly building
and the Polytechnic Institute,
near fashionable homes with hardwood floors,
the refugee camp lays itself down on its back
and groans,
a sick patient in need of life support.

II
What passes for home in the camp
is a depression in the ground
surrounded by four low mud walls.
The thin skin of a UNICEF tent
pulled over spindly bones
serves as a roof.
A sales brochure would emphasize highlands to the west,
rename this development Mountain View
and highlight the use of local materials and
        green construction techniques.

A neighbor, building one wall of a home, demonstrates.
From a rotting wheelbarrow
with cracked, bare, weathered hands,
he scoops dirt quarried nearby
and mixed with water at a community pump.
As a baker might with a lump of dough,
he flings the soggy mass of mud down
and flattens it
layer by layer
atop a rising, rectangular pile.

III
Four men lead us through a doorway cut in a mud wall
into an empty dirt courtyard
giving us a tiny measure of privacy.

We came to inquire and to listen,
but from the start we face questions:

You see how we live,
Mohammad says, gesturing toward his home.
Do you think it is comfortable here in winter?

Last year, all we had were tents.
We built these walls
to help protect us from the cold.

Mohammad asks other questions.
Who are you?
Why are you here?

And more subtly,
the question implicit.
Some people talk to us,
they take notes
and then never come back.
Nothing changes.

Six months ago, he tells us,
a reporter,
a British woman,
visited us.
While we spoke near the road, a motorcycle pulled up.
The driver shot her and sped away.
We carried her to a car
and they took her to a hospital.
But she came back.
She met with us again.

All of this by way of introduction
and negotiation.
A way of declaring:

We are people who need help.
We have nothing.
And you?
Do you trust what your own eyes tell you?

IV
News from Afghanistan
through the screen of embedded reporters
leaves behind the grit and grain of Afghan people.
The authoritative voice of the NPR reporter,
schooled in objectivity, balanced,
risking his life, serving his country's need for information.
But like a Pentagon press release,
everything begins with, revolves around, depends on
the US military
come to Afghanistan like a star,
like the sun,
the source,
the heavy weight spinning at the center
holding everything in check, in balance.

V
At Charahi Qamber,
a farmer from Helmand Province
pulled three crumpled photos from his dark, brown robe.
Images of destruction.
A home destroyed by a bomb.
A dead child lying on her back,
her stomach torn open.
Another child, a boy, also lying dead.

A Talib moved into the house next to mine.
A US plane, firing at him, hit our home.
The missile killed my wife and five children.

He stood there alongside three cousins,
their presence an indictment
unsealed, registered.

We left our farms, our livestock, our community,
one of his cousins said.
We came for our children's sake,
to bring them to safety.

He leveled his eyes at us.
I stood looking at him
no more than a stride away,
sure in the silence
that this was the voluble center of the universe.

We Knew

Charahi Qamber Refugee Camp
Kabul, Afghanistan
October, 2010

It has come to this.
Young American women and men—
mainly from poor families,
trained to kill,
paid to kill,
equipped with sophisticated weaponry
and shipped to foreign countries—
kill innocent children and adults,
mainly illiterate,
often people who never met an American before.
We call this fighting for democracy,
and national security.

Before we met Khalid,
before he reached like a parent into a pocket of his robe,
before his hand emerged with worn photos of his children
lying there torn, bloody, dead,
before the first assault of shock and horror gripped our throats
and shook us like rag dolls,
squeezing the air out of us

Before he told us,
an American missile destroyed my home
killed my wife and five children,

we knew that he was waiting for us in Afghanistan,
that he had left the lowland green fertility of his farm, his goats,
his village in Helmand,
left all but the memory of his wife and children
and come with his cousins to this brown, dusty, barren refugee camp

to live with nothing but a tent
between him and Kabul's mountainous winter.

We knew that others had come before him and others follow.
We knew that alarming numbers of American soldiers
home from Afghanistan
would beat their wives,
abuse their children,
kill themselves.

We knew this before Khalid's bearded face
and the broken faces of his children looked at us,
before the start of US military operations earlier this year
in Helmand Province,
before Barack Obama ordered a surge of troops,
before the first US troops arrived in Afghanistan in October of 2001.
We knew.

As Long As

Charahi Qambar Refugee Camp
Kabul, Afghanistan
October, 2010

As long as we have potatoes and wheat growing on our land,
sheep and goats grazing,
meat and bread and yogurt for our children,
let the Americans eat cake.

As long as we have electricity
and school children can study in the evening,
as long as our doctors have light in the surgery,
let the Americans play slot machines all night.

As long as we have clinics and hospitals,
let them build a Burger King on every corner.

As long as there is peace in our country,
as long as we can sleep at night,
let them plant vineyards,
let their rivers and reservoirs irrigate the vines.
As long as there are no American drones preying on us,
no American bombs driving us like animals from our homes,
let them build wineries.
As long as there are no American boots kicking in Afghan doors,
no Apache helicopters bombing Afghan homes,
killing Afghan children,
let them press grapes, drink wine.

But as long as packs of American Special Forces,
like wolves,
hunt us,
as long as American missiles seed our skies with knives and daggers,
our orchards with corpses,
as long as fear is the primary export to our country,

as long as our children learn the music and mathematics of killing
before they learn to talk,
let American wine be spilled;
let their rivers fail;
let their lakes and reservoirs turn to dust.

Let their children be seized with thirst
and let there be nothing to drink but blood.

In every American home,
only the blood of Afghan children.
In every room,
on every flat surface,
every table, desk, counter top, dresser,
a glass glowing with rich, red liquid.
In every family,
let their children wither,
let their lips crack, their tongues swell.
Let them drink blood.

They Give Themselves

Charahi Qamber Refugee Camp
Kabul, Afghanistan
October, 2010

In western Kabul,
the refugee camp is an expanding hole,
its walls crumbling,
unstable earth along its edges collapsing,
people falling in.
A hole without stairs or a ladder
without a rope from above.

On a visit to the camp,
Kathy and Jerica know what to do when meeting people
who have nothing.
They give themselves.

Jerica makes herself into a lap,
a pair of open arms,
a smile.
Children find her
and follow her.

Kathy disappears into a small, dark mud cave of a home
to be with a young mother who cannot come out,
who bursts into tears when they are in private.

As we are leaving,
two children fight,
the older girl coldly dragging the younger by a fistful of hair.
Blood, screams.
The cut is superficial
but below its surface, the emotional wound is raw.
Kathy kneels beside her,

smoothes her hair.
Jerica offers antibacterial ointment.
Kathy rubs it into the girl's forehead along her hairline,
the warmth of her touch traveling deep beneath the skin.

Restless Sounds

Charahi Qamber Refugee Camp
Kabul, Afghanistan
December, 2010

In December,
with warning words of a journalist friend

The camp is very dangerous . . .
kidnappers, thieves, gunmen . . .
best to avoid it . . .

still echoing in her mind,
Kathy and Asif return to Charahi Qamber refugee camp.

Other sounds echo.
Mohammad's voice, in October during Kathy's first visit,
People sometimes come here to ask questions,
but they don't come back.

In Afghanistan, the uneasy air vibrates with restless sounds.
Like sunlight absorbed and released by desert rocks,
sounds linger, reverberate.
A year after the fact,
Kathy can hear the long, deep-throated growl of the reaper drone
flying through thin air above Mohammad's village in Helmand
        Province.
Beneath everyday sounds in Kabul—endless traffic,
heavy machinery, the tumbling of locks, doors clicking open and
        closed—
Kathy hears the drone's missile wail as it tears through air.
She thinks she can hear its guidance system clicking
as it follows programmed coordinates to
        Mohammad's cousin's home,
the explosion when it lands, the splintering of
        furniture and bones.
She knows she can hear people wailing

when they find five children and their mother killed.
Though she hasn't heard him say so,
she believes Asif can hear it, too.

Having returned to Charahi Qamber,
Kathy now hears other sounds echoing.
Shy voices of nine-year-old Juma Gul and her brother
both injured in the missile attack.
The crunching underfoot of frozen dirt
as she bends and steps into their mud hut.
A small, metallic rasp as their father gently unzips Juma Gul's jacket.
The roaring silence within its sleeve
where Juma Gul's arm should have been.

Poetry

Kabul, Afghanistan
October, 2010

If poetry is a spontaneous surfacing from depths,
a release of something lighter than water
from muck and slime at the black bottom
of the wide river of our unconscious

If writing is paddling along its banks in starlight
to gather what is caught in low-lying branches
and roots of trees at water's edge
and to load it into a canoe
while cats prowl unseen
and snakes watch from branches overhead,
and later, in sunlight, to examine it

Then what is this sharp and polished bone
that rises in my throat and catches
every time we exit our guest house in a car
through the white, metal gate,
leaving armed guards behind
to enter the pulsing and chaotic sea of Kabul streets,
one more bite-sized fish darting out of its crevice
and joining the flow?

What is this blade I hold now in my hand in sunlight?
What is this blade that cut my larynx,
leaking blood into my lungs this morning at the IDP camp
when men from four families who live there
led us aside to a walled enclosure to speak,

families who have nothing,
who have seen the electricity to their futures cut,
the light extinguished,
farmers who have lost their land,

men and women who have laid children in graves
after US aerial bombardments?

Where was it made
and what can I learn from it,
this knife we call fear?

Street Girl

Kabul, Afghanistan
October, 2010

I
I'd read the statistics,
descriptive numbers rolled like runes onto blank pages
of important NGO reports
and carefully arranged,
a set of clear directions for travelers.

Nearly twenty-six percent of Afghan children die before their fifth birthday,
the highest rate in the world.

Fifty-nine percent are sufficiently malnourished
to be stunted mentally and physically.

Eight hundred and fifty children die every day
from preventable, treatable diseases
related to poverty.

But lacking imagination,
I never made the neural leap,
never found my way from faceless, black-and-white reports
to actual people.

II
Here in Kabul
on broken, unpaved streets,
organized packs of spindly, ragged children
move with vehicle traffic.

Like predators, they work their territory,
scanning the congested flow of cars
that occupies the streets like a slow-moving herd of horned beasts

and choosing vehicles with the weakest, likeliest passengers,
latching on to their prey by a door handle
and running alongside.

III
When we first meet,
her bony, dirty, brown face looks in the window
of our stationary car
as though we were seated at a restaurant
beginning a six-course meal,
steam rising into our faces as we leaned over bowls of hot soup.
Big, brown animal eyes only inches from my face.
She raps the window,
holds out her hand, widens her eyes and pleads,
Mister, mister
with a pathetic, exaggerated, practiced look.
I turn away.
The traffic jam eases
and our car leaps forward,
but she hangs on,
tapping the window with her fingernails and pleading.
Four or five minutes later,
after she has been dragged another half a block,
I find a scrap of my humanity,
reach into my pocket, open the car window,
and hold out a ten Afghani bill,
an embarrassingly small sum.
She snatches it with a bony hand
and disappears.

IV
Two days later, a flash of recognition at streetside
and she dances,
eager, hopeful,
through traffic to our car window.
This time, I manage a smile with the money.

V
The following day, we see each other
outside Spinney's,
a high-end grocery store where westerners shop
for everything from popcorn to mouth wash.
I smile as I walk out of the store.
She bounces.
But an Afghan man intercepts her,
blocks her approach,
scolds and warns her away from customers.
With a single, spontaneous movement of my head,
a simple lift of my chin,
I indicate *meet me up the road.*
Uneducated, illiterate, she reads me perfectly,
breaks away, and runs directly to the car window.
With over a week left in Kabul,
I am certain I'll see her again,
but it is the last time we meet.
I didn't even ask her name.

One Cup of Tea

Kabul Airport
October, 2010

A thin blade of frozen air
followed us into the open, unheated airport waiting room
and pierced our clothes—
cold hands, cold feet.

The air grew suddenly thinner and sharper
when Afghan police told me,
You cannot enter the terminal
without a paper ticket,
and the Kam Air sales representative couldn't access the Internet
to confirm our electronic reservations.

For a final time in Kabul,
an old, wooden door to unexplored, underground corridors
rattled in my mind
as fear fingered and shook its lock
and unwelcome images of being stranded in Afghanistan
escaped beneath the door.

How had we forgotten what country we were in
when we purchased the tickets online,
when we failed to print an electronic confirmation?

But Nasir, a one-man operation at Kam Air, wasn't daunted.
Twenty minutes later,
returning from the distant main terminal with a printout of our reservation,
he motioned me away from the walk-up window
and invited me into his cramped, dirty, dimly-lit office.
Turning on a propane heater, he asked, smiling
What do you think of our weather here in Kabul?
He ordered me a cup of tea,

shared cell phone pictures of his three young children,
and described Parwan Province—
mountainous, very beautiful—
the birth home from which his family fled violence.

I warmed my feet at the base of the heater,
wrapped my hands around the hot glass of green tea,
and listened.

Indigestion

Dubai, United Arab Emirates
October, 2010

I can't stomach this, Kathy says,
more than once,
referring to the indigestible contrast
between battered, dented, dusty Afghanistan
and polished, platinum Dubai

Between Kabul's pocked, pitted, unpaved, impassable, paraplegic
streets
and Dubai's wide, orderly avenues

Between the empty office buildings and dark homes in Kandahar,
waiting for electricity,
and Dubai's incandescent airport, business centers, hotels

Between night raids in Helmand
and the nights off in Dubai

Between illegal mud shacks climbing hills, circling Kabul,
without electricity, without plumbing, without sewers
and Dubai's glass and steel towers, its Olympian skyline

Between stunted, tatterdemalion, barefoot children
begging in the streets,
and Dubai's posh, private schools

Between marathon potato and wheat farmers in Bamiyan,
runners in a race without end,
and the golf courses, yacht clubs, casinos, and
        resorts in Dubai

Between the stone
and the pillow

Between the hard clay
and the hardwood floors

Between the hollow, haunted faces
and the averted eyes.

Unleashed

Kabul, Afghanistan
October-November, 2010

The US military has broken away,
drawn lines on maps,
fortified its presumptive borders,
and declared itself a sovereign nation.

No one can say precisely when it happened,
but in Afghanistan, evidence of it abounds.

In a long-planned assault
in farming villages along the Arghandab River
west of Kandahar,
in the Zhari District soldiers call the Heart of Darkness,
US Army crews are bulldozing trees and hundreds of houses, schools,
and mud grapevine trellises.
In double talk that reflects its breakaway status,
the military argues this destruction is a *positive development*
strengthening local government officials
who handle compensation claims.

Moving through the night,
in a policy one writer calls vigorous decapitation,
ten thousand US Special Operations forces are raiding Afghan homes,
removing the heads of Afghan families, binding their wrists and tying
black cloth hoods over their heads,
loading them like sheep into trucks,
and dragging them off.

While children watch,
armed foreigners erase their brothers, fathers, uncles,
violent images imprinted in the soft clay of their minds.
A military untethered,
unleashed,
accountable to no one.

Mathematics of War

Bamiyan, Afghanistan—US Skype conference call
November, 2010

War, Noor had told us,
is an expanding black hole at the center of our vision,
a macular degeneration.
Over time, the fine details are lost.
War puts people on the periphery
instead of at the core.

From his village
high in the central Afghanistan mountains
Lala provides one side of the mathematical proof.
Americans gathered at Saint Mark's Church in NYC
and on phones across the country
listen.

When I see American soldiers
with their big weapons,
I feel like my life does not matter.

And Brian, who served two years in Afghanistan
guarding the US embassy in Kabul,
proves the other side:

It is the same way for us.
When I was in Afghanistan,
I felt that the weapons were more important,
that they were valued more highly
than my life.

Followed

Bamiyan, Afghanistan
November, 2010

Every day since I met you, Abdulai,
since you greeted us at the edge of the
        United Nations landing pad
outside your home in Bamiyan,
you have pursued me.
Across continents and over oceans,
through language barriers,
on city subways and along mountain trails.

Behind all the poems,
while I wrote about visiting Mohammad Jan's
        family and about Faiz,
about Noor, Leila, Khalid
and a dozen other people we met in Kabul,
you were there,
the poetry like clouds in front of your sun.
Your small body attesting that four months of the year,
you have nothing but bread and potatoes to eat.
Your weathered hands bringing me back to your home,
to your mother telling us,
We age quickly here working in the fields
and *What we need is dignified work*
that will allow us to support our families.
Your voice telling Anees who is losing hope in
        Palestine, *Be strong.*
Your eyes asking for a chance, an opportunity,
a way to build
brick by brick
a world where you have a say.

Nothing Short Of

from Ukiah, California
November, 2010

after learning of the suicide of a US naval officer

In fact, no one saw it coming.
Maybe its indistinct shadow,
a smoky, broken image cast by dim light
on the uneven ground of a suck-it-up, military culture.
But not the real thing.
Not his hand
writing a suicide letter to his wife.
Not the six-word note
DON'T GO INTO THE CONFERENCE ROOM
pinned to his secretary's door
when she arrived at work that morning.
Not the looped rope
like a mouth open in horror
hanging in the air
beckoning him.
Not his feet stepping onto the chair,
his face and neck moving
breath by breath
toward that noose.

Of course, after his secretary found him dangling from the ceiling,
after they took down his body,
after the shock and awe,
a residue of guilt covered everything—

the furniture, rug, windows, walls,
even the beer bottles and Mai Tai glasses,
even the surfaces of dreams.

And nothing could have prevented this,
nothing short of actual troop withdrawal,

nothing short of never declaring war,
of never having stepped with a gun
into Iraq and Afghanistan.

Something to Say

En route Dubai to JFK
November, 2010

survivors of a US military attack speak out

We have something to say.

We were there when the Apache helicopters tracked
our three-vehicle convoy,
when they closed in and attacked,
unleashing their fanged weaponry
and killing people in the lead truck,
turning it into a heap of mangled steel.
Like wild dogs, the missiles tore at their dead bodies,
dragging pieces into the bushes to gnaw on.

We have something to say.
We were there when women and children in the next car
opened their doors and stepped outside.

We were there when they looked up
and women waved their head scarves
signaling *Civilians!* and *Don't shoot!* and *Call for help!*

We were sitting there
in horror
in the third vehicle
when the helicopters unleashed another missile
that shredded scarves and the hands that held them.

We have something to ask people in the US:
Do you think we are animals
to be hunted and killed?
Did the murder of our sisters and brothers and children
cause even a ripple
in the smooth pool of your conscience,

even a small interruption
in your routine,
in your pursuits?

We have something to say to the generals
and colonels and captains.
Words that survived in the smoke and rubble.
A few short sentences we found
while looking for the pieces of our family members,
while burying them.
Leave Afghanistan.
Dismantle your machines
and go home.

Why Not Listen

Kabul, Afghanistan
October— December, 2010

for Hakim

Despite razor wire, concrete barricades
and sandbags,
song birds are singing
outside Afghan government offices.
In the tree canopy,
sparrows and warblers.
And above them, whirling like acrobats,
swifts and swallows.

But the MPs inside cannot hear them.
Their songs have been replaced
by a rumble and thunder of warplanes.
Like earthquakes
with wave after wave of tremblers,
low-flying helicopters and airplanes rattle the offices
before landing at the nearby US Embassy.
As though the agitated air had hands.

But step outside.
The air carries other songs.

In Bamiyan, Hakim sings.
In Afghanistan,
forty-three countries mining for peace
tell us they have unearthed a treasure.
What is this treasure?
That violence can bring an end to violence.
But this is fool's gold.
Who decided that human beings are incapable of negotiation
and reconciliation?

Malalai Joya sings.
Democracy is not a commodity you can buy.
Peace is not a flower that Obama can give it to us.
Peace is the fruit of a long labor.
Labor with us, yes,
but another country cannot bring peace to Afghanistan.
Afghans will bring peace to our country.
We must find our own way to peace.

On the outskirts of Kabul,
in a dirt-floor tent where he works,
Member of Parliament Ramazon Bashardost sings.
Most Afghan people are saying something very simple.
"I am hungry."
Many young Afghan people work with the Taliban only to buy bread.

In Afghanistan, people do not want war.
But we are trapped.
Our leg is caught in a bear trap.
Obama is caught, too.
And slowly, we are bleeding to death
from the wound in our legs.
The trap is corruption,
a government run by warlords and drug traffickers.

Across the world, people know that elections in Afghanistan
were fraudulent,
but still Obama calls and congratulates Karzai.
We need tribunals
like those created in Lebanon and Africa,
a court with authority to stand up to the criminals.

Abdulai sings.
I wish to live without wars.

Every day in Kandahar City,

women risk their lives walking to work
at a local art cooperative.
Their refusal to be locked in their homes is a song.

Can you hear them?
Why not listen?

Seeking a Shore

Cairo, Egypt
the day after Hosni Mubarak resigned
February, 2011

I

In 2004, in the days after a tsunami spread its wide, heavy body
over Indonesia and Thailand and Sri Lanka and India,
crushing homes, hospitals, schools,
videos of the wave were posted online and shared electronically.
Accustomed to viewing explosions, raging waters, hurricane winds,
some people who watched videos online
from the dry comfort of their homes or offices were disappointed.
The wave didn't impress.
They would have been even more disappointed
had they followed the wave
as it moved through deep ocean waters,
only the crown of its head visible.
People failed to recognize its unity and dimensions,
how it had leapt from the sea floor,
gathered itself from so many individual particles of water
and traveled hundreds of miles
remaining intact,
how its legs extended deep into the ocean.

II

In Egypt, forcing the resignation of the dictator-president,
people have risen in a wave
and swamped the US-backed government of Hosni Mubarak.

A wave of humanity.
A wave of human longing.
Major media outlets are calling it an *18-Day Revolution,*
but it was decades in coming,
decades of resistance,
decades of people taking risks,

forming civil society groups,
speaking truth to their children
and nieces and nephews and neighbors,
decades of holding together.

And as tents were erected in Tahrir Square,
and we watched on Al-Jazeera and CNN and MSNBC and online,
we began to see how tall the wave is
and how long its legs are.

*I come from three generations who have been fighting for social reform
and fiscal freedoms in this country,* Khalid Abdalla said.

We watched as Hosni Mubarak tried to protect himself
by firing and replacing government ministers,
by bringing in a vice-president,
how, trying to prevent the waters from reaching him,
Mubarak laid down sand bags

only to see the wave come ashore outside the parliament building.
And it was too late to outrun it,
too late to seek high ground.

We watched in horror as Mubarak
tried to frighten people, to fracture and disrupt the wave,
as Egyptian police fired rubber bullets and tear gas
and turned water hoses on the protesters,
as pro-government groups, on horses and camels,
armed with sticks and rocks, and some, yes, some with guns,
charged Tahrir Square.
And three hundred people were killed.
And when the need for unity was greatest,
the wave held.

And awe, itself a wave, rolled over us.

III
Across the region,
in Iraq, Lebanon, Syria, Jordan, Afghanistan, Saudi Arabia, Yemen . . .
across the globe,
wherever the tectonic plate of government oppression
pushes against the rights of its citizens,
a shift occurs in people's hearts
and the same wave of longing leaps up to ride out on seas
seeking a shore.

"I come to Tahrir Square with my son after work every day," said Hossam Moussa, 41, an accountant. "I feel it's important for him to see for himself what it takes to build a better future."

—Bloomberg News, February 9, 2011

We Are Here to Stay

Cairo, Egypt and Bamiyan, Afghanistan
February, 2011

I

In Tahrir Square,
the rope and tarpaulin tents have tongues.
They cannot chant,
they cannot recite poetry or sing freedom songs,
but they are more than crude shelters.
Look, they say, *we are not leaving.*
Let all Egypt, they say,
let all the world know
we are here to stay.

II

Three months ago in Bamiyan, Afghanistan
a group of Afghan youth applied for a permit
to erect a "listening tent" in a Peace Park they helped create.
They wanted to invite Afghans to talk and listen.
They believe this is how they will find their way
out of a violent present into a peaceful future.
They wanted the tent to fill with words and with ears.
They wanted it to give birth to other tents in Bamiyan
and in other parts of Afghanistan.

Local officials denied their request
but they erected a tent anyway.
For five days, while three American activists visited them in Bamiyan,
they slept in the tent.
They filled it with their dreams.

I Cannot Hear the River Singing

Kunar Province, Afghanistan
March, 2011

Eleven-year-old Hemad speaks

I
We left our village together in the dark,
stars thick overhead.
Ten of us
all from the same village
following ancient footpaths
climbing along creeks into the mountains.
A thin blanket of silence lay over the Pech Valley,
the only sounds feet and hooves crunching,
our breath puffing.

II
We didn't know ourselves apart from that silence
and the vast spaces our mountains held in their hands
and a limitless sky above
leaning over us like a mother.

III
We'd known each other since before memory.
We liked being together.
In the mounting uncertainty of life in our village,
it was a comfort.

IV
Unarmed, leading our donkeys along the path,
we could not be mistaken for bandits, thieves, militants.
No one could see us for anything but what we were:
a group of boys awakened before dawn
and forced out under the stars by poverty and cold.

V

We'd done this hundreds of times.
Every rock and plant knew us.
In an ancient language,
the river sang songs of water locked in ice
and sunshine setting it free,
of Afghanistan's past and future,
and we thought we heard it murmur our names.
At night, as we slept,
these were the waters that invaded our dreams
and carried us away.

VI

But that day in early March
something else came to carry us away.
Something the music of the waters could not defend against.
A threat even its magic could not diffuse.

VII

Arriving, we spread out like a hand over the mountainside.
Like fingers, we combed the ravines,
bending and rising,
foraging for sticks and branches,
and piling them.
We trusted the trees and the soil.
We leaned against rocks to eat our lunch
and lay on the bare ground to nap.

VIII

We had come back together and were preparing to leave
when the helicopters flew overhead
and hovered above us.
Two of them
so loud they drowned the sound of the water.
We looked up,
and before the bullets struck us,

before the missiles tore through trees and exploded,
an instant before my friends were shredded and scattered like paper,
we saw a green flash.
It was the last light they saw.
Now it is the light I wake to in the morning
and the last thing I see at night.
And I cannot hear the river
singing.

Acknowledgments

This book owes its being to many people. I am deeply grateful to:

Marcia Gagliardi, the publisher, who guided and oversaw the entire production, for her enthusiasm, diligence, artistic sensibilities, and expertise during many rounds of editing

Copy editor Mary-Ann Palmieri for close readings of the text and skilled editing

Theresa Whitehill, of Colored Horse Studio, for her beautiful cover design and her encouragement

Photographer Tomiko Jones for use of her picture of Najlaa Al-Nashi

Filmmaker Sama Alshaibi for use of text from the beautiful movie, *The Rivers,* that she and Tomiko Jones filmed

Kathy Kelly for her friendship, her foreword, and her unfailing belief in a role for dramatic poetry in humanizing people from other cultures, educating us about the consequences of war, and pointing a way out of the modern morass of fear and violence

My wife, Sherrie Smith-Ferri, for her steady support, her artistic advice and help in selecting images for use in the book, and for sharing the risks of my travel to war zones

The Iraqi and Afghan people who trusted me, shared their thoughts and experiences with me, and welcomed me into their homes, and whose courage, resilience, and decency I tried to portray in these poems

The poems in this book would not have been written were it not for Kathy Kelly, Voices for Creative Nonviolence, and Direct Aid Iraq. To my co-workers and friends at these organizations, I am grateful: Jeff, Jerica, Gerald, Josh B., Dan, Mohammad, Josh S., Mary, Najlaa, Ghada, Rana, Mazen, Yasir, Noah, Arwa, Ben, Natalie, and Anna. Thank you to Hakim and to Ghada for their friendship and invaluable translating services. And thank you to Cathy Breen for sharing these poems with others and for her encouragement.

All proceeds from the sale of this book benefit the work of Voices for Creative Nonviolence. For more information, visit www.vcnv.org or contact the author at dsmithferri@gmail.com.

Poet David Smith-Ferri with Abdulai, a member of the Afghan
Youth Peace Volunteers
—photo by Jerica Arents

About the Author

David Smith-Ferri grew up in an Italian-Irish family in a suburb of
New York City. His mother's love for the literary and other arts and
her keen sense of justice shaped his sensibilities. As an undergraduate
at Boston College, participating in its service-learning program, he
worked in inner-city social service programs. He went on to get an
MSW from the University of Washington and to work as a social
worker in Seattle and New York. It wasn't until he and his then-five-
year-old daughter, Rachael, began visiting the Plowshares activist Susan
Crane in prison that he began to make connections between poverty
and social injustice in the US and American foreign policy. He has
been active with Voices for Creative Nonviolence (formerly Voices
in the Wilderness) since he first traveled to Iraq in 1999. Poetry has
played an increasingly important part of his activism as he has sought
effective ways to communicate the urgency of the problems he has
witnessed and to represent the voices of those who bear the brunt
of the US-led wars on Iraq and Afghanistan. His first book of poetry,
Battlefield without Borders, also published by Haley's, is in its second
printing. He lives in northern California with his wife and daughter. He
can be reached at dsmithferri@gmail.com.

Text, titles, captions, and other type for *With Children Like Your Own* are set in Gill Sans, a sans-serif typeface designed by Eric Gill.

The original design appeared in 1926 when Douglas Cleverdon opened a bookshop in his home town of Bristol, England, where Gill painted the fascia over the window in sans-serif capitals that would later be known as Gill Sans.

Gill further developed the font into a complete family after Stanley Morison commissioned the development of Gill Sans to combat the families of Erbar, Futura, and Kabel, launched in Germany during the late 1920s. Gill Sans was later released in 1928 by Monotype Corporation.

Gill was a well established sculptor, graphic artist, and type designer, and the Gill Sans typeface takes inspiration from Edward Johnston's Johnston typeface for London Underground, which Gill had worked on while apprenticed to Johnston. Eric Gill attempted to make the ultimate legible sans-serif text face.

The letter *a* was originally developed with a straight tail, followed by a diagonal tail (which can be seen on early specimen sheets), then the hooked tail.

The original Gill Sans lacked distinctions between numeral *1*, uppercase *i*, and lowercase *L*, so an alternate version of Gill Sans was made that included an alternate *1* that could be used for numerical settings.

Eric Gill removed terminus endings of the vertical stroke in *b, d, p,* and *q,* but the Monotype drawing office revised the forms so that they were preserved in the medium weight.

CPSIA information can be obtained at www.ICGtesting.com
264492BV00001B/19/P

9 781884 540288